GW00393457

THE
RETURNING
KING

THE
RETURNING
KING

A GUIDE TO THE BOOK
OF REVELATION

◆◆◆

VERN S. POYTHRESS

P&R
PUBLISHING
P.O. BOX 817 • PHILLIPSBURG • NEW JERSEY 08865-0817

© 2000 by Vern S. Poythress

All rights reserved. No part of this book may be reproduced, stored in a retrieval system, or transmitted in any form or by any means—electronic, mechanical, photocopy, recording, or otherwise—except for brief quotations for the purpose of review or comment, without the prior permission of the publisher, P&R Publishing Company, P.O. Box 817, Phillipsburg, New Jersey 08865-0817.

Scripture quotations are from the HOLY BIBLE, NEW INTERNATIONAL VERSION®. NIV®. Copyright © 1973, 1978, 1984 by International Bible Society. Used by permission of Zondervan Publishing House. All rights reserved. Italics in Scripture quotations indicate emphasis added.

Printed in the United States of America

Library of Congress Cataloging-in-Publication Data

Poythress, Vern S.
    The returning King: a guide to the book of Revelation / Vern S. Poythress.
      p.   cm.
    Includes bibliographical references and index.
    ISBN-10: 0-87552-462-1 (pbk.)
    ISBN-13: 978-0-87552-462-7 (pbk.)
     1. Bible. N.T. Revelation—Commentaries. I. Title.
    BS2825.3 P69 2000
    228′.07—dc21

                                            00-055808

Contents

The Appearing of Christ
  and the Final Battle (19:11–21)   173

Acknowledgments

This book is an expansion of study notes that I originally wrote for the *New Geneva Study Bible* (Nashville: Nelson, 1995). I am grateful to the Foundation for Reformation for permission to use my notes in expanded and altered form in this book, as a further aid to Christians who wish to appropriate the truths of the Word of God for themselves.

I wrote the bulk of this book before having in hand G. K. Beale's book, *The Book of Revelation: A Commentary on the Greek Text* (Grand Rapids: Eerdmans, 1999). I now find to my delight that Beale's approach is very similar to mine. He has provided the world with an outstanding technical commentary largely complementary to the practical focus of this book. Readers looking for more complete information and more thorough discussion may consult his commentary.

This book is dedicated to my wife, Diane, who has faithfully encouraged me to go forward with my writing and has given me many useful suggestions on how I may help us all "take to heart what is written in it" (1:3).

Introduction

Can We Understand Revelation?

Can the book of Revelation be understood? Yes, it can. Its message can be summarized in one sentence: God rules history and will bring it to its consummation in Christ. If you read it with that main point in mind, you will be able to understand it. You will not necessarily understand every detail—neither do I. But it is not necessary to understand every detail in order to profit spiritually from it.

The same thing is true of all Scripture. Scripture is inexhaustibly rich, so that we can never plumb all its depths and mysteries. But the main points are clear, so we can know what to believe and how to act (Prov. 1:1–7; Ps. 19:7–13). Second Timothy 3:16–17 tells us not only that all Scripture is inspired, but also that it is *"useful* for teaching, rebuking, correcting and training in righteousness, so that the man of God may be thoroughly equipped for every good work." All Scripture, including Revelation, has practical value for exhortation, comfort, and training in righteousness. Paul underlines this point in 2 Timothy 4:1–5 by drawing a contrast between the solid teaching of the gospel and people's desire to have teachers who "say what their itching ears want to hear" (4:3). God gave us Revelation not to tickle our fancy, but to strengthen our hearts.

The Clarity of Revelation

Revelation itself makes the same point in the first few verses, 1:1–3 (fig. 1). It is "the revelation of Jesus Christ." The word *rev-*

elation, or *unveiling,* indicates that it discloses rather than conceals its message. This revelation comes in order "to show his servants" something. The word "show" implies that the book can bring its message home to its hearers. Revelation is addressed to "his servants"—not just prophecy buffs, Ph.D.'s, experts, or angels, but *you.* If you are a follower of Christ, this book is for you and you can understand it. The third verse says, "Blessed is the one who reads the words of this prophecy, and blessed are those who hear it and take to heart what is written in it, because the time is near." God knew that some of his servants would hesitate over this book. So he gives extra encouragement to our reading by pronouncing an explicit blessing. Revelation is the only book in the whole Bible with a blessing pronounced for reading it![1]

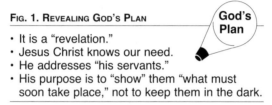

FIG. 1. REVEALING GOD'S PLAN

God's Plan

- It is a "revelation."
- Jesus Christ knows our need.
- He addresses "his servants."
- His purpose is to "show" them "what must soon take place," not to keep them in the dark.

But the reading should not be an empty or rote reading, as the continuation makes clear: "take to heart what is written in it." Revelation should not merely flit through our brain, or lead to vain speculations, but lodge in our heart and produce a practical response, a response of keeping it, just as we are to keep Christ's commandments by obeying them. (The Greek word *tereo,* translated "take to heart," is used in the Gospel of John for "keeping" Christ's commandments.)

Why the Confusion?

If Revelation is clear, why do so many people have trouble with it? And why is it so controversial? We have trouble because we approach it from the wrong end. Suppose I start by asking, "What do the bear's feet in Revelation 13:2 stand for?" If I start with such a detail, and ignore the big picture, I am asking for trouble. God is at the center of Revelation (Rev. 4–5). We must start with him and with the contrasts between him and his satanic opponents. If instead we try right away to puzzle out details, it is as if we tried to use a knife by grasping it by the blade instead of the handle. We are starting at the wrong end. Revelation is a picture book, not a puzzle book. Don't try to puzzle it out. Don't become preoccupied with isolated details. Rather, become engrossed in the overall story. Praise the Lord. Cheer for the saints. Detest the Beast. Long for the final victory.

FIG. 2. THE SIMPLICITY OF REVELATION

- Revelation is a picture book, not a puzzle book.
- It is for children also.

The truth is, some teachers of the book of Revelation set a bad example. They turn the book on its head; they turn it into a puzzle book. They preach obscurity instead of clarity, and of course people end up feeling incompetent.

Do the following responses sound familiar? "I'm confused." "It's so complicated." "I'm lost." "It's all a puzzle, and only this expert teacher can make sense of it." "I give up."

But a few refuse to give up. Instead, they develop an unhealthy preoccupation. They search for a complicated new scheme to "solve" the puzzle. They end up tickling the fancy and missing the real point.

In contrast, people who have not been influenced by superduper teachers do better with the book. Let me illustrate.

Once, when I was teaching Revelation, I noticed many children in the congregation. "I want you children to read Revelation, too," I said. "If you are too young to read it for yourself, have your parents read it to you. You too can understand it. In fact, you may understand it better than your parents."

A boy about twelve years old came up to me afterwards. "I know exactly what you mean. A short time ago I read Revelation, and I felt that I understood it."

"Praise the Lord!"

"I read it just like a fantasy, except that I knew it was true."

I thought, "Precisely."

This story was so good that I began using it when I taught Revelation in seminary classes. A student came up afterward.

"You know that twelve-year-old boy?"

"Yes."

"I know exactly what he meant. I can remember reading Revelation when I was about twelve years old, and understanding it. I have been understanding it less and less ever since!"

A group of seminary students finished playing basketball in a gym. They noticed the janitor in a corner, reading a book.

"What are you reading?"

"The Bible."

"What part of the Bible?"

"Revelation."

The seminarians thought they'd help this poor soul. "Do you understand what you are reading?"

"Yes!"

They were astonished. "What does it mean?"

"Jesus is gonna win!"

A charismatic pastor was praying in his study. "What should I preach on next?"

"Revelation."

"Great! I'll get out my seminary notes, dig in, whip up some diagrams, and show my stuff."

"No."

"What do you mean? What am I supposed to do?"

"Read it."

Pause. "That's crazy. I can't just stand up there and read it. Isn't a pastor supposed to teach? What good will I do?"

"Do it."

(Reluctantly) "O.K."

That congregation had the experience of a lifetime. The pastor dutifully read a paragraph. Then came responses: prayers, songs, praises, spontaneous exhortations, repentance for compromises with the world, and more praise. Then the pastor read another paragraph, and similar responses followed—and so they continued through the book. The congregation found that, taught by the Spirit of Christ, they did know how to understand! But if the pastor had gotten out those seminary notes and lectured, the congregation might have sunk into a puzzle-book mentality.

There is a lesson here. If you are leading a group in studying Revelation, do not become "the expert" in a bad sense. Yes, you can get help with the details by utilizing scholarly resources. And, yes, you can help people over some things that seem mysterious to a modern reader. But do it in a context where ordinary people can experience the book firsthand and follow its powerful drama for themselves, engaging their own hearts in the pictures (fig. 3).

Fig. 3. Encouraging Study of Revelation

Counterfeiting

We can illustrate how to understand Revelation by starting with one of its most important themes, the theme of spiritual warfare. Satan, the leader of the forces of evil, fights against God and the angels and God's people, but is ultimately defeated by the victor, Jesus Christ.

Consider the picture in Revelation 13:1:

> And the dragon stood on the shore of the sea. And I saw a beast coming out of the sea. He had ten horns and seven heads, with ten crowns on his horns, and on each head a blasphemous name.

Now there's a strange vision! But it is not quite so strange if we have already read about the Dragon in Revelation 12:3. The Dragon on the shore is a frightful monster. The Beast of Revelation 13:1–8 is likewise a monster. The Dragon has seven heads. The Beast coming out of the sea likewise has seven heads. The Dragon has ten horns. So does the Beast. The Dragon has crowns on his heads. The Beast has crowns on his horns. What is going on here?

The Beast is strikingly like the Dragon (fig. 4). In fact, he is an image of the Dragon. The Dragon stands on the shore of the sea in a way that is reminiscent of the Spirit of God hovering over the waters in Genesis 1:2. And then comes forth his "creation," the Beast, made in the image of the Dragon.

FIG. 4. THE BEAST AS SATAN'S IMAGE
AND ASSISTANT

Satan (12:3)	Assistant (13:1)
Pattern	**Image**
Dragon	Beast
7 heads	7 heads
10 horns	10 horns
Crowns on heads	Crowns on horns

Have we seen a process like this before? Of course we have. "God created man in his own image, in the image of God he created him" (Gen. 1:27). The Dragon is a picture of Satan (Rev. 12:9), who in Revelation 13:1 imitates what God did in Genesis 1:27. But what sort of imitation does Satan produce? It is not genuine, but counterfeit (fig. 5).

FIG. 5. THREE IMAGING RELATIONSHIPS,
ONE A COUNTERFEIT OF THE OTHERS

Pattern	Image
God the Father	Christ the Son (Col. 1:15)
God the Creator	Adam, God's created image (Gen. 1:27)

▲
Counterfeiting
▼

The Dragon	The Beast (Rev. 13:1)

Originally, God used imitation is a positive way. Man, as an image, reflected and displayed the character of God. In fact, imaging did not start with man! According to Colossians 1:15–16, even before creation the divine Son, the second person of the Trinity, was the image of God: "He is the image of the invisible God, the firstborn over all creation. For by him all things were created." The creation of man in God's image imitates the imaging relationship between God the Father and God the Son.

Now Satan is a counterfeiter. He counterfeits God the Father by producing a counterfeit "son," the Beast. The Beast is clearly the counterfeit of Christ the Son. Satan aspires to be God and to control everything for himself. He has a plan, analogous to the Father's plan. He will work out this plan through his executor, the Beast.

Is there then a counterfeit of the Holy Spirit as well? Yes there is, in Revelation 13:11–18. Another beast comes out of the earth (13:11). This beast is later identified as "the false prophet"

(16:13). The False Prophet works "miraculous signs" (13:13), reminiscent of the miraculous signs worked by the Holy Spirit in the book of Acts. Through miraculous signs, the Holy Spirit draws people to worship Christ. Analogously, the False Prophet promotes worship of the Beast (13:12). As "another Counselor," the Holy Spirit has the authority of Christ (John 14:16, 18). Similarly, the False Prophet "exercised all the authority of the first beast on his behalf" (Rev. 13:12). The Holy Spirit guides us into the truth (John 16:13). The False Prophet deceives (Rev. 13:14).

The Dragon, the Beast, and the False Prophet, therefore, form a kind of counterfeit trinity (fig. 6). They are linked together as a threesome when they organize people for the final battle (Rev. 16:13).

FIG. 6. A COUNTERFEIT TRINITY

Original	Counterfeit	Function
• The Father	• Dragon	Originate, plan
• Christ the Son	• Beast	Execute
• The Spirit as witness	• False Prophet	Witness, propagandize

The counterfeiting in Revelation can be demonstrated most impressively when we look at how the Beast counterfeits Christ (fig. 7). The Beast has ten crowns on his horns (13:1). In 19:12, Christ has "many crowns" on his head. The Beast has blasphemous names (13:1). Christ has worthy names (19:11–13, 16). The Beast has great power (13:2). Christ has divine power and authority (12:5, 10).

The Beast experiences a counterfeit resurrection. It seemed to have "a fatal wound," but the wound was healed (13:3). The counterfeit character of the Beast is clear in this feature. The Beast did not actually die and come to life again. He did not experience an actual resurrection. But he had a wound that one would think *should* have led to his death. His recovery was marvelous and astonishing—so astonishing that it was a big factor in leading people to follow him. Just as the resurrection of Christ is the chief event that astonishes people and draws them to follow him (John 12:32), so here a counterfeit miracle, a counterfeit resurrection, leads to people following the Beast.

There are still further parallels. The Beast receives worship (13:4), just as Christ receives worship (5:8–10). The worshipers offer a song of praise to the Beast: "Who is like the beast? Who can make war against him?" (13:4). This song blasphemously counterfeits the song offered to God at the Exodus: "Who among the gods is like you, O LORD? Who is like you—majestic in holiness, awesome in glory, working wonders?" (Ex. 15:11).

The Beast has a seal that is put on his followers (Rev. 13:16). In parallel fashion, Christ seals his followers with the seal of his name on their foreheads (14:1). At the last day, people from all nations will worship Christ (5:9), and he will exercise his authority over all. Meanwhile, the Beast "was given authority over every tribe, people, language and nation" (13:7).

The climactic confrontation between Christ and the Beast occurs in Revelation 19:11–21. Christ appears on a white horse, going out to war against God's enemies. The Beast appears as his chief opponent, leading the kings of the earth (19:19). The chief result of the battle is that the Beast and his assistant, the False Prophet, are defeated and consigned to the fiery lake (19:20).

In this scene, Christ is the divine warrior.[2] He fulfills the Old Testament prophecies that speak of God appearing to fight against the enemies (Zech. 14:1–5; 9:14–17; Isa. 59:16–18; Hab. 3:11–15). Christ is the holy warrior, who judges with justice (Rev. 19:11). The Beast, we infer, is the demonic counterfeit, the unholy warrior from the demonic region of the abyss. As Christ is the head of the holy army, so the Beast is the head of the unholy army.

FIG. 7. THE BEAST, A COUNTERFEIT OF CHRIST

	The Beast	Christ
Diadems	13:1	19:12
Name	13:1	19:11–13, 16
Power	13:2	12:5, 10
Resurrection	13:3, 12	
Worship	13:4	1:6
Praise	13:4	Ex. 15:3, 11f.
Seal	13:16	7:3; 14:1
Nations' allegiance	13:7f.	5:9

The picture of heading up a whole realm of followers recalls the idea of "federal" headship, that is, covenantal headship, expounded in 1 Corinthians 15:45–49. According to 1 Corinthians 15, there are two Adams, the first Adam and the last Adam. The first man, Adam, made from dust, is the pattern for all human beings descended from him. We too have bodies of dust, belonging to the earth. The last Adam, Christ, is the second man from heaven. He is the pattern for all human beings who are united to him, that is, all those who are under his federal headship. "Just as we have borne the likeness of the earthly man, so shall we bear the likeness of the man from heaven" (1 Cor. 15:49).

FIG. 8. THE WOULD-BE HEADSHIP OF THE BEAST

- Unholy vs. holy warrior (13:1–10 vs. 19:11–21).
- Two representative men (1 Cor. 15:45–49).
- The Beast as a third man, from the abyss.

Adam	Christ	The Beast
▼	▼	▼
Descendants	Christians	Followers

- His worshipers bear his mark (13:16; 14:9).
- He is a head representing a whole kingdom.

The Beast aspires to head up all nations (13:7–8). As a counterfeit of Christ, he aspires to be another federal head (fig. 8)! He would be a third man, from the abyss. The seal of his ownership in 13:16 then proclaims that his followers will be like him.

But note well that he is a *beast*, a hideous combination of lion, bear, leopard, and ten-horned monster. To be sure, the Beast as a symbol may possibly stand for a human being or a human institution in its rebellion against God. But it is no accident that it is represented as a beast. Although human beings may be involved, the thing is at root bestial. The tendency of the whole thing is subhuman, dehumanizing.

And that very fact is already an announcement of failure. The Beast cannot succeed, because he is bestial. Christ is not only "second" (1 Cor. 15:47), but "last" (1 Cor. 15:45). No one else can be a third after him, in the way that the Beast attempts to be. Genesis 1:28 indicates that the beasts are to be subordinate to Adam. And in the last days, the last Adam will make all beasts subject to him, including this great Beast (fig. 9). Christ wages war in Revelation 19, not only on behalf of God and his justice, but also on behalf of man and his welfare. He frees us forever from the threat of bestial tyranny. As the last Adam, he achieves perfect dominion. The Beast is subjected to Man.

FIG. 9. THE SUBJECTION OF THE BEAST

• Symbolically speaking, he is a beast.
• Beasts are destined to be subdued by man.

In Genesis 1	In Revelation 19
Adam	Christ
▼	▼
Animals	Beast

One other form of counterfeiting in Revelation needs to be mentioned. We have seen that an unholy trinity consisting of Satan, the Beast, and the False Prophet counterfeits the Holy Trinity consisting of Father, Son, and Holy Spirit. What about the worshipers of God? They are represented in Revelation 19:7–8 as the pure bride of the Lamb. Can Satan counterfeit the bride? He can and does. The counterfeit image of the bride is the Prostitute of Revelation 17–18. To the purity of the bride corresponds the corruption and immorality of the Prostitute.

The fall of the Prostitute becomes the occasion for the manifestation of the bride (19:1–6). Since the bride represents true worshipers, the true people of God, we infer that the Prostitute represents false worshipers, the counterfeit church.

FIG. 10. TWO OPPONENTS OF THE CHURCH

Satan	"Who will defeat God's people for me?"
The Beast	"I will."
The Prostitute	"I will."

Satan attacks the church directly through deceit and doctrinal confusion. He tries to turn the church away from the truth (12:15). But he also raises up underlings, in the form of the Beast and the Prostitute, who attack the church in specific, complementary ways (fig. 10). The Beast represents state power and threatens to persecute those who do not worship it. It attempts through threat, pain, and death to terrorize Christians into giving in to an idol. It stirs up fear of what will happen if you don't give in. We can generalize this tendency: we worship what we fear, whether the scorn of human beings, physical pain, or poverty. The remedy for this, of course, is the fear of God, which drives out the fear of man and of adverse circumstances.

But Satan also has another way of attacking. The Prostitute represents sex, money, and pleasure. Instead of threats and fear, she uses seduction and the lure of pleasure. Give in to your illicit desires. We worship what we desire, whether sex, money, health, long life, fame, or riches. The remedy for this is the desire to be in the presence of God in the new Jerusalem (Rev. 22:4). (See fig. 11.)

FIG. 11. HOW TO RESPOND TO BOTH FORMS OF OPPOSITION

Calling of the Church	Opposition	Response
Light-bearing witness	Persecuting power of the Beast	Endurance (13:10)
Virgin purity	Seductive luxury of the Prostitute	Separation (18:4)

Practical Lessons

We can immediately draw some practical lessons (fig. 12). Revelation shows that history involves spiritual war. In this war, there are two sides. You are either for God or against him. You either serve God or in one way or another will be found worshiping Satan and his bestial agents (cf. Rev. 13:7–8). Thus, Revelation implicitly issues a challenge like Joshua's: "Choose for yourselves this day whom you will serve" (Josh. 24:15). Giving our loyalty to God is absolutely crucial in determining the sort of life we have and the contribution that we make. Revelation reveals the crucial issues of life and the crucial destinies toward which life moves.

FIG. 12. LESSONS FROM COUNTERFEITING

- People are either for God or against him.
- Satan can only imitate God (2 Cor. 11:14).
  - There's a danger of believing the counterfeit.
  - Satan is not the Originator.
- We can see the repulsiveness of the counterfeit.
- A fit punishment for followers is to be under the Beast.
- God controls Satan (Job 1–2; Ps. 76:10; Rom. 8:28).

The fact that Satan engages in counterfeiting helps us to understand and prepare for spiritual war. Counterfeiting implies both danger and hope. The danger lies in the fact that Satan may fool people. The counterfeit is close enough to the truth to lure people into its grip.

But there is hope in the fact that Satan and his cohorts will surely be defeated. In fact, their defeat is implied by the facts about who they are. Satan aspires to be God. But he cannot succeed. He is not the creator or originator, but only an imitator. He is constantly dependent on God. Similarly, the Beast is bestial, and his kingdom must submit to the kingdom of the Man, the last Adam.

Revelation also gives us a key for escaping Satan's deceit. Although Satan continues to deceive the world, Revelation unmasks his devices in order to arm us to resist him. The world is in awe of the Beast and willingly worships him (13:3–4, 7). But when our eyes are enlightened by Revelation, we see how hideous he is. We may still be tempted to fear him because he looks so powerful. But, having seen him for what he is, can we honestly want to have him as our master?

Revelation shows not only the horror of following the Beast, but something of the consequences. In following Christ, the last Adam, we are conformed more and more to his image (2 Cor. 3:18; cf. 1 Cor. 15:49). By analogy, the followers of the Beast are in danger not only of being under his bestial tyranny, but of becoming bestial with him, since they bear his mark (13:16–18). It is like what the Psalms say of idolaters:

> Their idols are silver and gold, made by the hands of men. They have mouths, but cannot speak, eyes, but they cannot see. . . . Those who make them will be like them, and so will all who trust in them. (Ps. 115:4–8; cf. Ps. 135:18)

The punishment fits the crime.

Revelation uses irony in its depiction of God's opponents. Although they aspire to be like God, they end up being like beasts. Satan aspires to be the creator, but imitating the true Creator is already a confession of failure. Satan's resistance looks terrifying to the casual observer, but the person who probes more deeply sees that it is a miserable, stupid failure from beginning to end.

Finally, through its depiction of spiritual warfare, Revelation underlines an exceedingly important point: God is in control. He is in control not only of the general outline of history, but of its beginning, its end, and its details. He controls even the works of Satan for his own glory! The idea of God controlling evil and bringing good out of it occurs here and there in the Bible: Job 1–2; Psalm 76:10; Romans 8:28; Acts 4:25–28. It is clear in Job 1–2 that both God and Satan are actors behind the disasters that happen to Job (Job 1:12, 21–22!). Satan intends to destroy Job's faith and integrity and to disgrace the name of God as a result. God intends to magnify his own glory and cause Job's faith to grow through trial. Similarly in the crucifixion of Christ, according to Acts 4:25–28, Herod, Pontius Pilate, and the religious leaders perform their evil actions, filled with evil intent. But in those very actions, God accomplishes the salvation of the world. We do not comprehend fully how these things operate, but we can see that God's goodness and power are both absolute.

The same message comes out clearly in Revelation in pictorial form. Satan and his agents have impressive power and cleverness. Revelation does not conceal or minimize the reality of evil. The forces of evil, by their absolute opposition to God, and God's absolute opposition to them, underline the contrast between God's goodness and their evil. The warfare is real and bloody. But who is it that depicts the entire scene? Who is it that tells us not only what Satan is like, not only what he will in fact do, but what he *must* do because he has no alternative? It is God. God shows us the whole course of the warfare *beforehand*, thereby showing how thoroughly he controls the whole of history (cf. Isa. 41:21–29; 48:5–8).

Schools of Interpretation

We need now to sort out the major ways in which people have interpreted Revelation. Interpreters disagree concerning the period of time and the manner in which the visions of 6:1–18:24 are fulfilled. Four main approaches or schools of interpretation have developed over the centuries (fig. 13). *Preterists* think that fulfillment occurred at the fall of Jerusalem (if Revelation was written in A.D. 67–68) and/or the fall of the Roman Empire. *Futurists* think that fulfillment will occur in a period of final crisis just before the Second Coming. *Historicists* think that 6:1–18:24 offers a basically chronological outline of the course of church history from the first century (6:1) until the Second Coming (19:11). *Idealists* think that the scenes of Revelation depict principles of spiritual war, not specific events. These principles are operative throughout the church age and may have repeated embodiments.

FIG. 13. TIME OF FULFILLMENT ACCORDING
     TO THE SCHOOLS OF INTERPRETATION

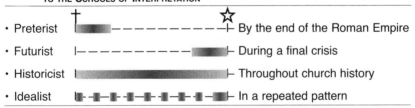

• Preterist	By the end of the Roman Empire
• Futurist	During a final crisis
• Historicist	Throughout church history
• Idealist	In a repeated pattern

We can illustrate the differences by considering how people interpret Revelation 13:1–8. When and how does the imagery of

the Beast find fulfillment? Preterists see in the Beast the persecution of Christians by the Roman emperor. Futurists see the future Antichrist, the man of lawlessness of 2 Thessalonians 2:3–12.
Historicists find here the pope, who persecuted the Reformers.
(But some Roman Catholic historicists would say that Martin
Luther is pictured!) Idealists think of the state and its persecuting
power whenever and wherever it rises to threaten Christians.

Or again, consider the vision of the locust plague in 9:1–11.
Preterists say it "symbolizes the hellish rottenness, the internal
decadence in the Roman Empire."[3] Historicists associate it with
the Islamic invasion of the West. The crowns of verse 7 are the
turbans of the Arabs.[4] The breastplates of iron in verse 9 stand
for "the steel or iron cuirasses of the Arab warriors."[5] The five
months (v. 10) are 150 years, from 612, the public opening of
Mohammed's mission, to 762, the removal of the Caliphate to
Baghdad.[6] The matches here may seem impressively detailed, until one realizes how many dates and details might have been
searched to make things work.

For Seiss, a futurist, all the material is a literal description of
future agents of judgment.[7] For Hendriksen, an idealist, it a generalized picture of how the wicked suffer for their wickedness:
"Can you conceive of a more frightful and horrible *and true(!)*
picture of the operation of the powers of darkness in the soul of
the wicked during this present age?"[8]

A combination of these views is probably closest to the truth.
The imagery in Revelation is multifaceted, and is in principle
capable of multiple embodiments. Idealists maintain that general principles are expressed. If so, those principles had a particular relevance to the seven churches and their struggles in the
first century (1:4; see "Occasion and Purpose" below). The principles also will come to climactic expression in the final crisis of
the Second Coming (22:20; cf. 2 Thess. 2:1–12). We ourselves
are involved in the same spiritual war, and so we must apply the
principles to ourselves and our own time (see the note on 1:3).
Hence, many passages have at least three main applications,

namely to the first century, to the final crisis, and to us in whatever time we live.

Let us consider the main points in favor of each of the four main approaches. If more than one approach seems appealing, it confirms that a multifaceted fulfillment is probably right.

Insights from Idealism: Repeated Pattern of Fulfillment

What indications in Revelation favor an idealist approach?

What we have already seen of satanic counterfeiting favors idealism. On a basic level, Satan's methods are always the same. He must be an imitator of God, because he is not the Creator or originator. Since God is always the same, satanic counterfeiting will always be the same.

Moreover, as we shall see in examining the structure of Revelation, the appearing of God in chapters 4–5 is at the heart of the book. God's character is at the bottom of all the visions, and it determines in profound ways what John sees. Revelation is about theophany, God appearing. God appears climactically and finally at the time of the Second Coming. But even now he rules from his heavenly throne and is present with us. The manner of his rule and presence is determined by who he is in heaven. Hence, there is a common theological character to the entire age. Moreover, God's action now has a similar structure to his climactic appearance, in conformity with the general New Testament pattern of "inaugurated eschatology." Through Christ's resurrection and the gift of the Holy Spirit, we are sons of God right now (Rom. 8:14–17). At the Second Coming, we receive sonship in its fullness (Rom. 8:23). In union with Christ, we have resurrection life now (Col. 3:1). At the Second Coming, we will have resurrection bodies (1 Cor. 15:50–56; Phil. 3:21).

Several more minor points support the idea that Revelation intends to describe the entire period between the First and Second Coming of Christ:

- Revelation is addressed to "his servants" (1:1; 22:6), thereby including all Christians in all locations and times (22:18).
- The seven churches in chapters 2–3 stand for all churches everywhere. Other churches in the same region (at Colossae and Hierapolis) are not mentioned. It appears that seven churches are selected because the number seven symbolically represents completeness. The refrain near the end of the message to each church is "He who has an ear, let him hear what the Spirit says to the churches" (2:7, 11, 17, 29; 3:6, 13, 22). "He who has an ear" includes in principle any Christian. The plural word *churches* suggests that people ought to listen to all the messages, not merely the one immediately addressed to their church. Hence, the messages are applicable generally, and this generality would include even those beyond the membership of the seven churches together—not only people at Colossae and Hierapolis, but in any location and at any time.
- The fluidity and multifaceted character of symbols opens the way to seeing multiple applications.
- Revelation 4:1 and 1:1 indicate that Revelation is unfolding the period of "last things" (eschatology) included in Daniel 2:45, which encompasses the entire period between the First and Second Coming of Christ.[9]

Revelation 4:1, referring to "what must take place after this," has exactly the same words in Greek as Daniel 2:45 (Theodotion's translation). Similar wording, "what must soon take place," opens Revelation in 1:1. There are further subtle connections. In Daniel 2:45, God shows the king what must take place. In Revelation, God shows his servants what must take place. In Daniel 2:45, "the dream is true and the interpretation is trustworthy." In Revelation 19:11 (cf. 1:5), Christ is called "Faithful and True" (using the same Greek words). Nebuchadnezzar's dream in Daniel 2 sets out the course of history. After a succession of godless world empires, the kingdom of God comes in the time of the fourth empire, the Roman Empire (2:40–44). Daniel includes both the inauguration and the consummation of God's kingdom in a very brief description (2:44). Thus, the entire age between the First Coming of Christ (when the kingdom of God was inaugurated during the period of the Roman Empire) and the Second Coming (when the kingdom will be consummated) is included.

All of this eschatological action was hundreds of years distant from Daniel's own time. John, on the other hand, found himself right in the middle of the action. What was distant for Daniel was therefore "soon" for John—indeed, it was already beginning to take place before his eyes.

Note also that God designed Scripture to be applied:

- Since all Scripture is profitable (2 Tim. 3:16–17), so is Revelation. Since Revelation is part of Scripture, it applies to us.
- In view of 2 Timothy 3:16–17, even if one of the other schools of interpretation is correct, Revelation must also have an application for us. To do so, it must generalize beyond the particular circumstances of the first century (preterism) or the final crisis (futurism). The generalized truth that it uncovers will match the idealist's viewpoint. Hence, in terms of application for today, any of the four approaches tends to yield roughly the same results as an idealist approach.

Insights from Futurism: Fulfillment in the Final Crisis

What indications in Revelation appear to favor futurism?

Revelation looks forward above all to *the* great event of Christ's coming:

- The celebration at the marriage supper of the Lamb (19:6–9) and the appearing of Christ to fight the final bat-

tle (19:11–21) seem unmistakably to point to the Second
Coming.

- The vision of the new Jerusalem in 21:1–22:5 shows a perfection that lies on the other side of the Second Coming
  (see 21:8, 27; 22:4–5).
- The "time" in 1:3 is the time when Christ comes, according to 22:10–12.
- The Second Coming is described in 1:7: "Every eye will
  see him."
- The final promise, "Yes, I am coming soon" (22:20) refers
  to the Second Coming.

The liturgical response, "Amen. Come, Lord Jesus" (22:20),
reiterates the prayer of the early church, "Come, O Lord!" (1 Cor.
16:22), originally in Aramaic (*Marana tha*). The church knew
that Christ might "come" in a sense to have fellowship with them
in the Lord's Supper, and that he might "come" to execute judgment on unbelief as in the fall of Jerusalem (Luke 21:20–24). But
we cannot exclude from this prayer the reference to the most ex-
citing, climactic, and desired coming of all, the great coming
when he appears (1 Thess. 4:13–5:11). The Second Coming was
the great hope of the early church, and first-century Christians
would have read Revelation with that hope in mind.

Insights from Preterism: Fulfillment in the Roman Empire

What indications appear to favor preterism (fulfillment in the
Roman Empire)?

The strongest evidence for a preterist approach lies in the connections of Revelation with the situation of the seven churches.
Every one of the messages in chapters 2–3 contains details about
the first-century church situation, including subtle allusions to the
wider environment in the city (see the commentary on chapters
2–3 and Colin Hemer's *The Letters to the Seven Churches of Asia*).
The problems addressed in chapters 2–3 continue to be in focus

throughout the rest of the book. The visionary material of 4:1–22:5 has many links with chapters 2–3. For example, references to "those who say that they are Jews and are not" (2:9; cf. 3:9) are connected with the vision of the true Jews in 7:1–8. Satan's throne in 2:13 relates to the Dragon (Satan) in 12:9. Martyrdom in 2:10, 13 links up with martyrdom in 6:9; 11:7; 13:15; 17:6; 20:4. The promise of the tree of life in 2:7 is linked to the tree of life in 22:2. Jezebel in 2:20–22 ties in with the Prostitute of chapter 17. Through these and other linkages, it becomes clear that the whole book, not just chapters 2–3, addresses the problems and struggles of the seven churches in the first century.

Other arguments also favor preterism:

- Revelation is apocalyptic literature (see "Apocalyptic" below), and, according to many scholars, all apocalyptic literature is about its own time, not the distant future.

But this argument rests on a fallacious generalization. In the Bible, Numbers 23–24, Ezekiel, Daniel 7–12, Isaiah 24–27, Zechariah, 1 Thessalonians 4–5, 2 Thessalonians 1–2, the Olivet Discourse (Matt. 24; Mark 13; Luke 21), and Revelation are examples of apocalyptic literature (see "Apocalyptic" below). All of these passages were designed to have practical value for the immediate audience, but often by giving predictions of the distant future. One may also find predictions of the future in extrabiblical apocalyptic, such as the Qumran War Scroll, 1 Enoch, and 4 Ezra.

- The time is near (1:1, 3; 22:10).

"The time" in question must be the time in which most of the visions find fulfillment. It is not adequate to interpret this language as affirming merely a theoretical imminence of the Second Coming. It is true that no one knows the exact time of Christ's coming (Mark 13:32–37; Acts 1:7). The "we" language in Paul shows that, as far as he knew, Christ might return while he was still alive (1 Thess. 4:13–5:11; 1 Cor. 15:51). That is to say, Christ's coming *may* be near; it *may* be soon. But Revelation 1:3 and 22:10 assert that the time *is* near. They offer us a confident assertion, not a statement of possibility.

Nearness of the Time

The assertion of nearness might seem to be in tension with the arguments in favor of futurism. If the time of fulfillment includes the Second Coming, how can it be "soon" and "near"? This question is so vexing that it deserves separate attention. Interpreters have offered several solutions.

- According to many modernists and unbelievers, John was wrong. He predicted that the Second Coming would occur soon, but it did not.

This solution is unacceptable. It denies the divine authority of the Bible and judges itself wiser than God, just as Satan has always tempted us to do (Gen. 3:1–5).

- The beginning of the fulfillments is near, because 6:1–3 receives its fulfillment soon.

But 1:3 and 22:10 are like bookends enclosing the whole prophecy of Revelation. The fulfillment of everything, not just a part, is near.

- The "coming" of Christ that Revelation anticipates is not the Second Coming, but various "comings" before the End in order to punish or reward. Note the mention of Christ coming in 2:5, 16; 3:11.

But in reply we may say that 2:5, 16 and perhaps 3:11 have contexts that limit or even redefine the kind of "coming" in view. Such limitations are not present in 1:7; 22:20; and 21:1–22:5.

- The Second Coming is imminent (*may* be near).

But see the discussion of preterism above for the problems with this approach. To say that we do not know the time is not the same as saying that it is near.

- The "nearness" is a structural nearness belonging to the whole period of inaugurated eschatology, from the First Coming to the Second.

The connection with Daniel 2:45, discussed with regard to idealism above, seems to point in this direction. What is distant from Daniel's point of view is now near—indeed, already in process. Moreover, neither Old Testament prophecy nor New Testament prophecy is preoccupied with lengths of time as measured by the clock. They focus more on the character of the times. Jesus' exhortations to watch (Mark 13:32–37) do not depend on whether the Second Coming is five days away or five millennia away, but on the responsibility of his disciples after he, the master, "leaves his house."

One may see a similar attitude in 1 John 2:18: "Dear children, this is the last hour." For John, it is not only the last days, but the last "hour"! How can John say that? Has he received a special notice from God about the length of time left? By no means. He expects rather to convince his readers of this truth by appealing to facts that they already know: "As you have heard that the antichrist is coming, even now many antichrists have come. This is how we know it is the last hour."

John's hearers already knew about the Antichrist, in the singular. He is probably to be identified with the man of lawlessness in 2 Thessalonians 2, whom Christ destroys at the Second Coming (2 Thess. 2:8). Such wicked opposition had been predicted in the vision of the little horn of Daniel 7:8, 20–22 (cf. 8:9). John then observes that there are many antichrists, in the plural. In their function, these belong in the same broad category with the final Antichrist (cf. 2 Thess. 2:7). They show that we are living in times that are structurally like the final crisis, when the singular Antichrist will be revealed. They show that we are already in the period of Daniel's little horn, a period that, from an Old Testament prophetic point of view, is the last hour before God's judgment (Dan. 7:22).

The nearness in Revelation needs to be interpreted in the same way. Revelation describes throughout its pages the character of the interadvental period. This period, according to Daniel, lies just before the final judgment (see above on idealism).

Think of a carnival. People using a sledgehammer try to propel a weight up to hit a bell at the top. The rising of the weight is like the rising of a crisis of persecution and antichrist activity. The weight gets near to the top, that is, near to the Second Coming. It may rise and fall several times before someone finally succeeds in ringing the bell. Likewise, there may be many crises before the end, and each is near to the Second Coming.

Insights from Historicism: Fulfillment Spread Linearly Through Church History

Of the four schools of interpretation, historicism is undoubtedly the weakest, though it was popular centuries ago. With preterism, it correctly sees that Revelation begins with the situation of the seven churches. With futurism, it correctly sees that Revelation ends with the Second Coming. It also notices that Revelation moves toward a climax, that there is a drama of development as one reads through the book. So it simply stretches a time line from the first century in Revelation 2–3 to the Second Coming in 19:11–21, and tries to correlate the visions in between with the events of world history.

But in the process it assumes that the visions in Revelation portray events in chronological order. In fact, however, the order of the visions is thematic, not simply chronological, as one can see from 12:5 (see "Structure" below). Hence, the historicist approach, insofar as it assumes a strict chronological order, must be abandoned.

Combining the Insights of the Schools

All the schools except the historicist school have considerable merit. Can we somehow combine them? If we start with the idealist approach, it is relatively easy to see how. The images in Revelation enjoy *multiple* fulfillments. They do so because they embody a general pattern. The arguments in favor of futurism show convincingly that Revelation is interested in the Second Coming and the immediately preceding final crisis (cf. 2 Thess. 2:1–12). But fulfillment in the final crisis does not eliminate earlier instances of the general pattern. We have *both* a general pattern *and* a particular embodiment of the pattern in the final crisis.

Likewise, the arguments in favor of preterism show convincingly that Revelation is interested in the seven churches and their historical situation. The symbols thus have a particular embodiment in the first century, and we ought to pay attention to this embodiment.

Finally, we have a responsibility to apply the message of Revelation to our own situation, because we are somewhere in church history, somewhere in the interadventual period to which the book applies. Here is the grain of truth in the historicist approach.

We can sum up these insights in a single combined picture. The major symbols of Revelation represent a repeated pattern. This pattern has a realization in the first-century situation of the seven churches. It also has an embodiment in the final crisis. And it has an embodiment now. We pay special attention to the embodiment now, because we must apply the lessons of Revelation to where we are.

Content and Style

How can we best summarize the overall content of Revelation? In the opening vision, Christ appears as the majestic king and judge of the universe, and as ruler of the churches (1:12–20). In 2:1–3:22, Christ addresses specific needs of each church. His powerful promises also remind the churches of the scope and profundity of their calling (2:7, 10–11, 17, 26–28; 3:5, 12, 21). The selection of exactly seven churches suggests the wider relevance of the message (see the commentary on 1:4).

In 4:1–22:5, Christ's rebukes and encouragement take a new form. Through Christ and his angels (22:8–9, 16), John receives a series of visions intended to open our eyes to the kingship and majesty of God, the nature of spiritual warfare, God's judgments on evil, and the outcome of the conflict. God and his army will win the battle (17:14; 19:1–2), but his forces are powerfully opposed by Satan, the great Dragon (12:3), who leads the whole world astray (12:9). Satan has two agents, the Beast and the False Prophet, who together with him make up a counterfeit trinity (13:1–18; 16:13; see the note on 13:1–10). The Beast, representing raw power and state persecution, threatens to suppress true witness and compel people to worship him (13:7–8). The False Prophet is his assistant and propagandist. Babylon, representing the worldly city and the desirable aspects of idolatrous society, threatens to seduce the saints away from spiritual purity (2:20–23; 17:1–18). In opposition to these threats, the saints must maintain their testimony, even to the point of martyrdom (12:11), and must maintain their spiritual purity (14:4; 19:8). In the consummation, their witness finds its fulfillment in the final light of God's truth (21:22–27), and their purity is fulfilled in the spotless bride of the Lamb (21:9).

The principal theme of Revelation is that God rules history, and that he will bring it to its consummation in Christ. At the center of the book are the visions of Christ (1:12–16) and of God (4:1–5:14). God displays his majesty, authority, and righteousness as the ruler and judge of the universe (see the commentary on 1:12–20). These central visions foreshadow the consummation of history, when God's glory will fill all things (21:22–23; 22:5; see the commentary on 4:1–5:14). Detailed elements in the visions flesh out these truths, and are to be seen as part of a larger picture.

Major Themes

A number of major themes run through the book. We discussed satanic counterfeiting above. But there are many other important themes that interlock with this one.

God. Revelation is first of all God-centered. God controls the course of history. He protects his people and punishes rebellion. He will bring his purposes to final, spectacular realization in the new heaven and the new earth.

Worship. The appropriate response to God on the part of his creatures is worship. Scenes of worship occur throughout the book (1:12–20; 4:1–5:14; 7:9–17; 8:3–5; 11:16–19; 12:10–12; 14:1–7; 15:2–8; 16:5–7; 19:1–10; 20:4–6; 21:1–22:5). By showing us the marvel of who God is and what he does, Revelation calls us to respond with awe, godly fear, praise, faith, and obedience. Thus, all of Revelation promotes true worship of God.

The Lamb. In the realization of God's purposes, the Lamb has the key role (5:1–14). Jesus Christ is presented to us as the

Lamb to symbolize his sacrificial death. His deity is shown by the fact that he shares God's names (the Alpha and the Omega, the First and the Last, 1:8, 17; 22:13), his throne (22:1), his attributes (1:13–16 compared to Dan. 7:9–10), and his worship (5:13). Only through the Lamb, by virtue of his death and resurrection, can God's plan for history be unrolled (5:1–10). The Lamb mediates God's judgments in history (6:1; 19:11–21).

Visions. God discloses his purposes in visionary form (1:12–22:5), sometimes accompanied by sounds and verbal messages as well. Symbolic figures and scenes indicate the relation of God's plan to history. The symbolic form of communication seems strange to many modern readers, but it was familiar to people in the first century. Revelation belongs to a larger pattern or genre of communication called apocalyptic (see "Apocalyptic" below).

Theophany (God's appearing). Revelation presents its concerns in visionary form. It is fitting, then, that at the thematic center of all the visions stands the vision of God himself. He appears enthroned in the midst of his heavenly angelic assistants in 4:1–11. He appears when Christ appears in 1:12–16. He appears climactically at the close of this age, at the Second Coming. All the events of this age move forward toward the Second Coming. Revelation contains a dramatic momentum that increases as we approach that great event.

In fact, in a broad way theophany controls the entire contents of Revelation. It is important not to rush by the descriptions of God appearing, in order to get to the details of prophecy. The main point is right there in who God is. The details are consequences that derive from who he is.

We can see the centrality of God's appearing as we travel through the main sections of the book. God appears through the appearing of Christ in 1:12–16. Christ is the announcer of the messages to the seven churches in chapters 2–3. Moreover, each message begins with an allusion to the character of Christ as revealed in chapter 1. All but the last two of the messages refer to some feature from the vision in 1:12–20. For example, at the beginning of the message to the church at Ephesus, Christ says, "These are the words of him who holds the seven stars in his right hand and walks among the seven golden lampstands" (2:1). He is referring to the stars in 1:16 and the lampstands in 1:12. The last two messages, to Philadelphia and Laodicea, show more distant connections. The "key of David" in 3:7 is similar to the "keys of death and Hades" in 1:18. The "faithful and true witness" of 3:14 corresponds to the "faithful witness" of 1:5.

The vision of God in 4:1–5:14 is the key opening scene from which the action of the book unfolds. Subsequently, we find that there are seven cycles of judgment, each of which leads up to the Second Coming (see "Structure" below). The first of these cycles consists of the opening of the seven seals, 6:1–8:1. The seals belong to the heavenly book that appears in 5:1. The Lamb, who appears in 5:6, is the one who opens the seals. Thus, the action in 6:1–8:1 is controlled by the Lamb and the sealed book from the vision in 5:1–14. The judgments issue from the presence of God.

The other cycles are similarly dependent on the appearing of God and his presence, although the kind of dependence is not always immediately obvious. The cycle of seven trumpets is set in motion by seven angels "who stand before God" (8:2). Hence, these judgments issue from the presence of God.

The cycle of symbolic histories in 12:1–14:20 has as a major focus the counterfeit trinity, consisting of the Dragon, the Beast, and the False Prophet. These three counterfeit the activity of the Trinitarian God (see "Counterfeiting" above). As such, they are dependent on God. Their appearance is a hideous counterfeit of his appearance.

The cycle of seven bowls in 15:1–16:21 issues from the temple of God (15:5–8). The temple is "filled with smoke from the glory of God and from his power" (15:8), a sign of his presence in theophany.

The next cycle, in 17:1–19:10, focuses on Babylon, the counterfeit of the bride in 19:7. The bride reflects the glory of God in theophany (see 21:9, 11). Babylon is a counterfeit of this appearing.

The cycle with the rider, in 19:11–21, is an appearance of Christ, who is the divine warrior (see "Counterfeiting" above).

The unit in 20:1–15 focuses on scenes of heavenly rule (20:4, 11–15), which involve theophany.

The vision of the new Jerusalem in 21:1–22:5 has at its center "the throne of God and of the Lamb" (22:1), who are seen by the worshipers (22:4).

Thus, theophany functions as a kind of origin for the symbolism of Revelation 1:12–22:5. Indeed, all that visionary material can be thought of as a giant, complex theophany, together with its accompaniments.

Spiritual War. Revelation goes beneath the surface in its analysis of history in order to show the spiritual forces at work. God and his agents war against Satan and his agents. Humanity is in the middle of this war. One's allegiance to God or to Satan, and the consequences in one's life, structure the meaning of history (see "Counterfeiting" above). By adopting this spiritual perspective, Revelation does not eliminate human responsibility and the significance of human action, but rather sets them in their final, cosmic, and theistic context. It thus provides a powerful antidote to secularism. And it offers as well a powerful antidote to false religions, by showing us what is at stake. False religion can be blatantly non-Christian, like Hinduism or Islam. Or it can be a corruption of true Christianity, like classic Roman Catholicism, modernism, legalism, or nominalism.

Bipolar Contrasts: Purity and Corruption, Beauty and Ugliness, Truth and Deceit. The focus on spiritual war alerts us to the polarity between good and evil. To eyes that are morally and religiously sleepy, things look very confused. And, indeed, human beings often walk in a kind of moral twilight of mixed motives, where one seldom sees clearly the complex entanglement of good and evil motives in a single attitude or action. Revelation acknowledges that existing situations are often painfully confused and frustratingly mixed (chapters 2–3). But it does so not to excuse us and to permit a lapse into moral complacency, but in order to stir us up to undivided allegiance to God and the Lamb. For this purpose, stark contrasts between purity and corruption, beauty and ugliness, and truth and deceit run through the book. The difference between God's ways and Satan's ways touches on every aspect of life, whether it be purity, singleness of heart, moral action, aesthetic issues (beauty and ugliness), or cognitive issues (truth and error).

Witness and Martyrdom. The theme of witness runs through the book. John *"testifies* to everything he saw" (1:2). He has "the *testimony* of Jesus Christ" (1:2). Jesus is "the faithful *witness"* (1:5) in a special, preeminent sense. Revelation contemplates a situation where Christians are subject to persecution for their faith (see "Occasion and Purpose" below). They may even be subject to the death penalty if they maintain their witness faithfully (2:10, 13; 13:15). Jesus Christ was martyred because of his faithfulness to God. Christians may face the same fate. But if so, they share also in Christ's victory over death (1:18). Revelation can be seen as one great call to faithfulness, even to the point of death (2:10).

Reward and Punishment. Faithfulness to Christ makes sense, even if we must pay a price for it. Revelation points to the fact that God is sovereign and just. He punishes rebels and rewards his faithful followers. The punishments and rewards include both the preliminary judgments in history, short of the Second Coming, and the final judgments at the Second Coming itself. Even though the saints may seem small, weak, and defeated in human eyes, full vindication is coming in God's own time.

Apocalyptic

In its style and content, Revelation shows tantalizing similarities to some other writings in the Bible and to others outside the Bible as well. Especially during the period from about 200 B.C. to A.D. 400, various "apocalyptic" writings appeared. Among them were the War Scroll from Qumran, the Assumption of Moses, 1–2–3 Enoch, 2–3 Baruch, 4 Ezra, the Apocalypse of Peter, the Apocalypse of Paul, the Apocalypse of Thomas, and the Ascension of Isaiah. Within the Bible, apocalyptic features are apparent in Numbers 23–24, Daniel, Ezekiel, Isaiah 24–27, 1 Thessalonians 4–5, 2 Thessalonians 1–2, the Olivet discourse (Matt. 24; Mark 13; Luke 21), and Revelation.

Leon Morris helpfully summarizes the main features of apocalyptic writing:[10]

1. Revelation of the secret things of God, inaccessible to normal human knowledge. Secrets of nature, of heaven, of history, of the end.
2. Pseudonymy (the real author writes in someone else's name, such as Enoch or Ezra).
3. History rewritten as prophecy.
4. Historical determinism, ending in cosmic cataclysm that will establish God's rule.
5. Dualism (good and evil).
6. Pessimism about God's saving rule in the present.
7. Bizarre and wild symbols denoting historical movements or events.

But "apocalyptic" is a loose category. Not all the writings share all the features. Revelation shares some, but not all, of these features. And even those features are modified. Let us consider the above points one by one.

1. Revelation does offer a "revelation of the secret things of God." But a deeper analysis shows that very little in Revelation is completely new. It repeats in symbolic form the message of the rest of the New Testament. Few of the "secrets" that it reveals are, to Christian believers, otherwise inaccessible.

2. What about pseudonymy? Outside the Bible, we find writings like 2 Baruch and 4 Ezra, which pretend to contain secrets revealed to Baruch or Ezra, but which were actually composed long after their death. By contrast, Revelation comes simply from "John" (Rev. 1:1) (see "Author and Date" below). It is not pseudonymous. It does not pretend to be something it is not.

3. Revelation does not report history as if it were prophecy. It is forward looking.

4. Revelation does present us with a kind of determinism: God controls the entirety of history. Moreover, history leads up to a final cataclysm and the renewal of heaven and earth (21:1). But there are subtle differences. In Revelation, God's determinism is not fatalism. During this age, Christian obedience is important (e.g., 2:5, 7, 10–11, 16–17). Earnest exhortation is an important part of the book, unlike some apocalyptic writings.

5. Revelation does contain an ethical dualism between good and evil, but this dualism is not frozen or fatalistic. Through repentance, people can cross from evil (death) to good (life) (22:17).

6. Pessimism about God's saving rule in the present is absent. Although the conflict is fierce, victory belongs not only to the future, but even to the present, because the Lamb has already triumphed (5:5; 12:10–12).

7. Bizarre and wild symbols dominate the main visionary section of Revelation. But while these symbols may seem bizarre and wild from a modern point of view, they are not bizarre from the point of view of the original readers. Revelation introduces very little that is entirely new. Rather, it combines and reworks symbols that are already present in earlier parts of the Bible, and

occasionally it adopts common symbolism from outside the Bible as well.

A good deal of the uniqueness of Revelation arises from one central point. Revelation is a Christ-centered vision. Christ is the way to God; he is the mediator of God's plan for history. The truthfulness of Christ's witness, and the fact that Christ is the truth incarnate, make inappropriate the use of the "pious fictions" of pseudonymy and history-as-prophecy (points 2 and 3). The openness of Christian revelation makes irrelevant any preoccupation with secret knowledge (point 1) or bizarre, novel symbolism (point 7). The determinism and dualism of Revelation (points 4 and 5) are both qualified by the fact that Christ's death and resurrection introduce the great epoch of salvation. The gospel spreads to the nations and invites people everywhere to participate in salvation rather than remain under God's wrath. The pessimism of extrabiblical apocalyptic writing is inappropriate because Christ has already triumphed (point 6).

Hence, we must not expect too much from comparisons of Revelation with extrabiblical apocalyptic literature. We learn mainly one thing: the use of complex symbolism was "in the air" at the time when John was writing. It would not have seemed as strange then as it does now.

Some people today come to Revelation with the recipe, "Interpret everything literally, if possible." That recipe misunderstands what kind of book Revelation is. Of course, John literally saw what he says he saw. But what he saw was a vision. It was filled with symbols, like the Beast of 13:1–8 and the seven blazing lamps in 4:5. It never intended to be a direct, nonsymbolical description of the future. People living in John's own time understood this matter instinctively, because they recognized that John was writing in an "apocalyptic" manner, a manner already as familiar to them as a political cartoon is to us today.

Author and Date

The human author identifies himself simply as John (1:1, 4, 9; 22:8). He was well known to the churches in Asia Minor (1:4, 11; see "Occasion and Purpose" below). As early as the second century A.D., Justin Martyr, Irenaeus, and Clement of Alexandria identified the author as the apostle John.[11] The testimonies of Justin Martyr and Irenaeus are particularly weighty. Justin lived for some time at Ephesus in the early second century, among those who still remembered John. Irenaeus was in his youth a disciple of Polycarp in Asia, and Polycarp was a disciple of John.

In the third century, however, Dionysius, bishop of Alexandria, compared the style and themes of Revelation with the Gospel of John and concluded that the two must have had different authors. Modern scholars discern the same differences, and so various hypotheses have arisen to throw doubt on Justin's and Irenaeus's testimony. On balance, it is still probable that the apostle John was the human author.

Revelation stresses that its message and content derive ultimately from Jesus Christ and from God the Father (1:1, 11; 2:1; 22:16, 20). It possesses full divine authority (22:18–19). This divine authority, rather than the identity of the human author, remains the most significant foundation for interpretation. Even if Revelation had a different human author from the Gospel of John and 1–2–3 John, it shares themes with these writings of John and hence invites comparison with them. On the other hand, even if all these writings have the same author, Revelation belongs to a different genre. Hence, it must be appreciated in its special character and not be assimilated too quickly to John's other writings.

When was Revelation written? It was written when persecution was impending (2:10, 13). In the figure of the Beast, Revelation alludes to the fact that in the Roman Empire, subject peoples were expected to worship the emperor as a god. Refusal to participate in such worship seemed to express political disloyalty. Hence, we may ask when in the first century such persecution took place. That would give us an idea of when the book was written.

Irenaeus says that Revelation was written near the end of the reign of the Roman emperor Domitian (81–96).[12] In later centuries, the church thought of Domitian as one of the worst persecuting emperors. While he was reigning, he claimed divinity and was addressed as "god and lord." But in the earliest sources, it is unclear how far his demand for worship was enforced.

The other attractive date is at the end of the reign of the emperor Nero (54–68). In the early years of his reign, competent advisors had great influence, but things degenerated in his later years. He is notorious for having blamed Christians for the fire of Rome in 64. He used this accusation as an excuse to persecute them. But again, there is no clear evidence that this persecution ever extended beyond the city of Rome. It is much more important to know what was going on in Asia Minor among the seven churches. Concerning the situation there, we have little information beyond what Revelation itself gives us.

Some interpreters think that Revelation 11:1–13 and especially verse 8 predict the fall of Jerusalem that took place in 70. Hence, Revelation would have been written shortly before that, perhaps in the last years of Nero's reign (about 66–68). But 11:1–2 is symbolic of the church, not the temple of stone in

Palestine (see the commentary). Verse 8 is also symbolic. Hence, these verses do not really decide the date one way or the other.

Revelation 17:10 is often cited in favor of a Neronian date. It says that the seven heads of the scarlet beast (17:3) "are also seven kings. Five have fallen, one is, the other has not yet come; but when he does come, he must remain for a little while." In agreement with preterism, and in agreement with God's concern for the seven churches, it is appropriate to interpret this statement with reference to its first-century setting. The Beast represents the Roman Empire in its idolatrous claims. The heads may therefore be successive emperors. Julius Caesar was the first emperor, followed by Augustus, Tiberius, Caligula, Claudius, and Nero. Nero is therefore the sixth, which fits perfectly with 17:10. But there are several difficulties with this approach:

- Does Revelation's reckoning begin with Julius Caesar or with Augustus?

Among Roman and Jewish writings, one can find writers beginning with either.[13]

- Can one harmonize the history after Nero with a reckoning in which Nero is the sixth king?

After Nero came Galba, Otho, and Vitellius, who fought for control of the Empire in 68–69. Vespasian reigned from 69 to 79, Titus from 79 to 81, and Domitian from 81 to 96. Even though 68–69 was a time of confusion, Galba, Otho, and Vitellius all "held the office and title of emperor,"[14] and later historians include them in the lists. The climactic character of the seventh and eighth kings must clearly correspond to something more dramatic than Galba and Otho.

- The "five who have fallen" may not be five successive Roman emperors.

They may instead be five successive world-dominating *empires:* Egypt, Assyria, Babylon, Medo-Persia, and Greece. The sixth, the one who "is," is then the Roman Empire in its totality. But it seems that the Beast of 17:3 and 13:1–8 is the Roman Empire rather than all the empires combined. Hence, it is more likely that five is a symbolic number. By saying that the sixth one "is," Revelation indicates that the final crisis, to take place with the seventh and climactic head, is just around the corner. Six is the number to choose in order to say that we are almost but not quite at the end. Five has no other significance than the fact that it is one less than six.

We have one piece of information from the Roman historian Suetonius that may help to date the onset of the most serious persecution. In his book *Domitian,* Suetonius reports:

> Besides other taxes [under Domitian], that on the Jews was levied with the utmost rigour, and those were prosecuted who without publicly acknowledging that faith yet lived as Jews, as well as those who concealed their origin and did not pay the tribute levied upon their people.[15]

What is the significance of this note? Because of financial problems in his central administration, Domitian looked carefully for all possible sources of revenue. He enforced all the taxes that were already "on the books," but which may have fallen into disuse. Among these was a head tax of two drachmas levied on the Jews. Before the fall of Jerusalem, money gathered from this tax was used for the upkeep of the temple in Jerusalem. But after the destruction of Jerusalem, it went to the temple of Jupiter Capitolinus in Rome.[16] Jews paid this tax as an alternative to emperor worship.

The Roman administration understood that Jews were monotheists, and they were exempt from the normal requirement to show political loyalty to the Empire by emperor worship. But Christians were in danger. In the early days of

Christianity, Roman officials would have regarded Christians as a Jewish sect (cf. Acts 25:19). But as the number of Gentile Christians multiplied, this classification seemed less and less appropriate. When Domitian began to enforce the tax, the status of Christians would naturally come up for investigation. Moreover, non-Christian Jews who were at enmity with the church may have denounced Christians to the Roman authorities, saying, "These people claim to be Jews, but they are not." Hence, they would have been suspected of disloyalty to the Empire, and subjected to enormous pressure, including possibly violent persecution. The possible role of Jewish denunciations may illumine the meaning of the statements in Revelation about "those who say they are Jews and are not, but are a synagogue of Satan" (2:9; cf. 3:9).

Thus it seems probable that there was persecution in the time of Domitian. This time fits best with the situation described in Revelation.

Occasion and Purpose

Revelation is addressed to seven churches in Asia Minor (1:4, 11), which is today part of western Turkey. Each church receives rebukes and encouragement, in accordance with its condition (2:1–3:22). Persecution has fallen on some Christians (1:9; 2:9, 13; 3:9), and more is coming (2:10; 13:7–10). Roman officials would try to force Christians to worship the emperor. Heretical teachings and declining fervor would tempt Christians to compromise with pagan society (2:2, 4, 14–15, 20–24; 3:1–2, 15, 17). Revelation assures Christians that Christ knows their condition. He calls them to stand fast against all temptation. Their victory has been secured through the blood of the Lamb (5:9–10; 12:11). Christ will come soon to defeat Satan and all his agents (19:11–20:10), and his people will enjoy everlasting peace in his presence (7:15–17; 21:3–4).

Structure

Revelation has some characteristics of apocalyptic literature (see "Apocalyptic" above). Like Ezekiel, Daniel, and Zechariah, it contains visions with many symbolic elements. Using visual imagery as well as verbal promises and warnings, it weaves together into a poetic tapestry the themes of the rest of Scripture. Its depths are displayed through the multiplicity of its allusions.

What are the major divisions of the book of Revelation? The prologue of Revelation (1:1–3) explains its basic purpose. The rest of the book is a letter with greeting (1:4–5a), body (1:5b–22:20), and farewell (22:21). This is the same formal arrangement as in Paul's letters.

A clue for dividing up the main body of the book is provided in 1:19. "What you have seen" refers to the vision that John has already experienced (1:12–20). "What is" refers to the present state of the churches (2:1–3:22). "What will take place later" refers to the future-oriented section in 4:1–22:5. The propriety of this threefold division is confirmed by the close match between "what will take place later" in 1:19 and "what must take place after this" in 4:1 (in Greek, only one word differs). This threefold division, however, is only a rough one. The section 2:1–3:22 contains future-oriented promises, and 4:1–22:5 contains much information relevant to the present situation of the churches.

How do we proceed to divide the large section from 4:1 to 22:5? Interpreters continue to disagree on the proper divisions.

Revelation is like a tapestry, with many interwoven patterns. Choosing one pattern as the basic one may lead to an outline of one type, while choosing a different pattern leads to a different outline. It is wiser, then, to recognize that no one outline or structural analysis captures everything. We here present several outlines and structures, each focusing on a different aspect of the total pattern.

We may begin with a focus on "formal," grammatical patterning. Repeated phrases give us clues. The visions accompanying the opening of the seven seals belong together. Likewise, the seven trumpets belong together. Less obviously, major shifts of scene are indicated when John is transferred to a new location. Each such transfer takes place "in the Spirit," and in each case (after the first) there is the statement, "I will show you. . . ." Using these clues, we obtain the following outline:

Formal Clues

    I. Prologue, 1:1–3
   II. Introduction of the letter, 1:4–5a
  III. Body of the letter, 1:5b–22:20
       A. Opening, 1:5b–8
       B. Middle, 1:9–22:17
          1. Introduction, 1:9
          2. Visions, 1:10–22:5
             a. Vision of Christ, 1:10–3:22
                (1) The meeting with Christ, 1:10–20
                (2) Messages to the churches, 2:1–3:22
                    (a) Ephesus, 2:1–7
                    (b) Smyrna, 2:8–11
                    (c) Pergamum, 2:12–17
                    (d) Thyatira, 2:18–29
                    (e) Sardis, 3:1–6
                    (f) Philadelphia, 3:7–13
                    (g) Laodicea, 3:14–22
             b. Vision in heaven, 4:1–16:21
                (1) Throne vision, 4:1–11
                (2) Scroll, 5:1–14
                (3) Seven seals, 6:1–8:1
                    (a) First seal, 6:1–2
                    (b) Second seal, 6:3–4

Now let us take a second, complementary approach. In this second approach, we look at content rather than formal clues. The most important event toward which history moves is the Second Coming. Visions that describe it mark important transitions. When we go to Revelation with this concern in mind, we find descriptions of the Second Coming no less than seven times! There are seven cycles of judgment, each leading up to the Second Coming. A final, eighth vision shows the new Jerusalem, the consummate state on the other side of the Second Coming. Here is the resulting outline:

Rhetorical Structure

   I. Prologue, 1:1–3
  II. Greeting, 1:4–5a
 III. Body, 1:5b–22:20
     A. Thanksgiving, 1:5b–8
     B. Main part, 1:9–22:5
       1. What you have seen, 1:9–20
       2. What is, 2:1–3:22
       3. What is to be, 4:1–22:5
         a. Cycle 1: seven seals, 4:1–8:1
         b. Cycle 2: seven trumpets, 8:2–11:19
         c. Cycle 3: symbolic figures and the harvest, 12:1–14:20
         d. Cycle 4: seven bowls, 15:1–16:21
         e. Cycle 5: judgment of Babylon, 17:1–19:10
         f. Cycle 6: white horse judgment, 19:11–21
         g. Cycle 7: white throne judgment, 20:1–21:8
         h. The eighth and culminating act: new Jerusalem, 21:9–22:5
     C. Final instructions and exhortations, 22:6–20
  IV. Closing salutation, 22:21

The cycles parallel one another. All cover the same period leading up to the Second Coming. But each cycle does so from its own distinct vantage point. Moreover, later cycles concentrate more and more on the most intense phases of conflict and on the Second Coming itself.

We may summarize the focus of the different cycles as follows:

Commission
- Seven seals, 4:1–8:1. Commission of covenant judgment in heaven. The origin of God's triumph.

Prosecution of War
- Seven trumpets, 8:2–11:19. Effects on earth.
- Seven symbolic histories, 12:1–14:20. Depth of conflict.
- Seven bowls, 15:1–16:21. Effects on earth, further intensity.

Elimination
- Seven messages of judgment on Babylon, 17:1–19:10. Elimination of the seductress.
- White horse judgment, 19:11–21. Elimination of the power source.
- White throne judgment, 20:1–21:8. Elimination of all evil.

Now we can look in greater detail at each cycle of judgment. In the cycle of seven seals and in the cycle of seven trumpets, we see a common pattern. First, John sees an opening scene, which depicts the origin of the judgments that will take place during the cycle. Then come six successive judgments. Then we have an interlude, focusing on a message of promise and comfort for the saints. Then follows the seventh judgment. The judgments are predominantly negative in character, but the interlude is predominantly positive. The origin of the judgments is both positive and negative—a source of punishment for rebels and a source of comfort for saints. The structure can be represented as a pattern of *a, b, a', bb*. The *a* part is positive while the *b* part is negative. The double *bb* at the end represents a final, more intensive judgment. The prime on *a'* indicates that it is distinct from the original *a*.

1. Cycle 1: seven seals, 5:1–8:1
   a. Scene: the recompenser, 5:1–14

      b. Six judgments, 6:1–17
      a´. Promise for the church, 7:1–17
      bb. Seventh judgment, 8:1
  2. Cycle 2: seven trumpets, 8:2–11:19
      a. Scene: the recompensers, 8:2–6
      b. Six judgments, 8:7–9:21
      a´. Promise for the church, 10:1–11:14
      bb. Seventh judgment, 11:15–19

Since this pattern is so clear in the first two cycles, it is natural to try to detect it in the remaining cycles. We obtain the following as a more complex analysis:

  I. Introduction: the participants, 1:1–11
  II. Body: the message, 1:12–22:5
    A. The judge, 1:12–20
    B. Preliminary promises and warnings for the churches, 2:1–3:22
    A´. Judgment on the world, 4:1–21:8
      A. Scene: recompenser-creator, 4:1–11
      B. Six cycles of judgment, 5:1–19:21
        1. Cycle 1: seven seals, 5:1–8:1
          a. Scene: the recompenser, 5:1–14
          b. Six judgments, 6:1–17
          a´. Promise for the church, 7:1–17
          bb. Seventh judgment, 8:1
        2. Cycle 2: seven trumpets, 8:2–11:19
          a. Scene: the recompensers, 8:2–6
          b. Six judgments, 8:7–9:21
          a´. Promise for the church, 10:1–11:14
          bb. Seventh judgment, 11:15–19
        3. Cycle 3: seven symbolic histories, 12:1–14:20
          a. Scene: two poles; the woman and the Dragon, 12:1–6
          b. Six symbolic histories, 12:7–14:11
            (1) The Dragon's history, 12:7–12
            (2) The woman's history, 12:13–17
            (3) The Beast, 13:1–10
            (4) The earth beast or False Prophet, 13:11–18
            (5) The 144,000, 14:1–5
            (6) The angelic proclaimers, 14:6–11
          a´. Promise for the saints, 14:12–13
          bb. Seventh symbolic history: the harvest of the Son of Man, 14:14–20
        4. Cycle 4: seven bowls, 15:1–16:21

   a. Scene: the recompensers, 15:1–8
   b. Six judgments, 16:1–14:16
   a′. Promise for the church, 16:15
   bb. Seventh judgment, 16:17–21
  5. Cycle 5: seven messages of judgment on Babylon, 17:1–19:10
   a. Scene: symbolic actors (recipients), 17:1–6
   b. Six messages of destruction, 17:7–18:19
    (1) First angelic message, 17:7–18
    (2) Second angelic message, 18:1–3
    (3) Third heavenly message, 18:4–8
    (4) The kings of the earth, 18:9–10
    (5) The merchants, 18:11–17
    (6) The seafaring men, 18:18–19
   a′. Promise for the saints, 18:20
   bb. Seventh message of destruction, 18:21–24
   a″. Sevenfold joy in heaven, 19:1–10 (19:1–2, 3, 4, 5, 6–8, 9, 10)
  6. Cycle 6: the white horse judgment, 19:11–21
   a. Scene: the recompenser, 19:11–16
   b. Angelic message of destruction, 19:17–18
   a′. Promise for the saints, 19:19c
   bb. Final judgment of the Beast and the False Prophet, 19:19–21
 A′. Promise for the saints, 20:1–10
  a. Scene: the recompenser, 20:1
  b. Preliminary judgment, 20:2–3
  a′. Promise for the saints, 20:4–6
  bb. Final judgment of opponents and Satan, 20:7–10
 BB. Cycle 7: the white throne judgment, 20:11–21:8
  a. Scene: the recompenser, 20:(7–10,) 11
  b. Divine judgment, 20:12–15
  a′. Promise for the saints, 21:1–7
  bb. Exhaustive judgment, 21:8
𝓑𝓑. Final promised blessing of the consummation, 21:9–22:5
III. Concluding remarks and exhortations, 22:6–21

In addition to these patterns, still other patterns exist in the form of chiasms, that is, mirror-image patterns.

Symbolic personages are introduced into the drama one by one, and then their destinies are assigned in the reverse order, as follows:

A. The people of God depicted with the imagery of light and creation, 12:1–2
  B. The Dragon, Satan, 12:3–6
    C. The Beast and the False Prophet, 13:1–18
      D. The bride: the people of God in the imagery of sexual purity, 14:1–5
        E. Babylon the prostitute, 17:1–6
        E. Babylon destroyed, 17:15–18:24
      D. The bride is blessed with marriage, 19:1–10
    C. The Beast and the False Prophet are destroyed, 19:11–21
  B. The Dragon is destroyed, 20:1–10
A. The people of God in the imagery of light and creation, 21:1–22:5

Chiastic Thematic Structure: Especially War

There also seems to be a major chiasm involving themes:

A. Leading into the visions: the seer, the revealers, and the audience, 1:1–11
  1. Prologue, 1:1–3
    a. Title, 1:1a
    b. The witness, 1:1b–2
    c. Reading the prophecy, 1:3   Guarantee of victory
  2. Participants, 1:4–11
  B. Christophany, 1:12–20
    C. Recompense to the churches: the church militant, 2:1–3:22
      D. Throne vision, 4:1–5:14
        E. Seven seals: rider judgments (1–4 focus on humans), 6:1–8:1
          1. Content of the judgments, 6:1–17
          2. Preservation of the church, 7:1–8:1
        F. Seven trumpets: angelic judgments (1–4 focus on nature), 8:2–11:19   Judgments on men and nature
          1. Judgment on the nations, 8:2–9:21
          2. Preservation of the church, 10:1–11:14
          3. Joy in heaven, 11:15–19
        G. The redeemed, 12:1–6   Victors in strife
          (with intermixed strife, 12:3–6)

H. Deceptive opponent
(Satan), 12:7–17

   I. Destructive opponent
      (Beast), 13:1–10   Villain

H. Deceptive opponent
(False Prophet),
13:11–18

G. The redeemed, 14:1–20   Victors
(with intermixed strife,   in strife
14:6–20)

F. Seven bowls: angelic judgments
(1–4 focus on nature), 15:1–19:10

   1. Judgment on the nations,
      15:1–16:21

   2. End of the false church   Judgments
      Babylon, 17:1–18:24   on nature
   3. Joy in heaven, 19:1–10   and men

E. White horse: rider judgment (focus on
humans), 19:11–20:10

   1. Content of judgment, 19:11–21

   2. Preservation of the church,
      20:1–10

D. Throne vision, 20:11–15

C. Announcement of recompense to the
churches: church triumphant, 21:1–8

B. Theophany, 21:9–22:5

A. Leading out of the visions: the seer, the revealers,   Enjoying
and the audience, 22:6–21   the victory

   2. Participants, 22:6–17   and its

   1. Epilogue, 22:18–21   fruits

     c. Reading the prophecy,
        22:18–19

     b. The witness, 22:20

     a. Colophon, 22:21

Many other thematic features unify the book (see "Major Themes" above). Repeated use of the number seven signifies completeness. God's plan and power determine the outcomes. Praise to God rises from the angels and from the saints (see the note on 1:6). Satanic counterfeits oppose God in a spiritual war of cosmic proportions. The present struggles of the church (2:1–3:22) contrast with its final rest. The church must maintain its witness and its purity. Everything moves forward to the victory of Christ at his coming.

Commentary

A Heavenly Vision (1:1–20)

Prologue (1:1–3)

The main portion of Revelation (1:4–22:21) has the form of a letter (see "Structure" in the Introduction). The section 1:1–3 functions as its prologue. It helps to orient readers to the kind of contents they may expect. Stress is placed on the divine authority of the message (from God and Jesus Christ), its certainty ("must" in v. 1), and its crucial importance (v. 3). God makes thorough provision for the communication process: the message originates with God the Father, is given to Jesus Christ, and is made known to John through an angel (v. 1). John testifies by writing that message (v. 2), and all are encouraged to read and hear it (v. 3).

Although Revelation comes in symbolic form, it is understandable. It is "revelation," disclosing rather than hiding truth (v. 1). It is for "his servants," not a special elite (v. 1). God expects us to "take to heart what is written," to profit spiritually (v. 3). A blessing encourages people to read and hear it (v. 3).

The book identifies itself as **the revelation of Jesus Christ.** This expression might mean a revelation with Jesus Christ as its *source.* Or it might mean a revelation with Jesus Christ as its principal *content.* Both possibilities express important truths.

Two factors weigh decisively in favor of the first meaning (Jesus Christ is the source). First, the immediate context in 1:1–3 focuses on the means and channels of revelation. God the Father is the ultimate source, Jesus Christ is the mediator, he sends "his angel," John writes the message, and others read it aloud. Second, although the book does indeed have a sustained Christological focus, the content is more broadly Trinitarian and not narrowly Christological. The focus is also on what happens in history. The events are mediated by Christ, but they can still be distinguished from him.

How can the events take place "soon" (v. 1), if nearly two thousand years have passed since John wrote (see also 22:6–7, 10, 12, 20)? The answer is that spiritual war takes place throughout the church age, and that the seven churches will soon experience all the dimensions of the conflict. Moreover, "the last days" foretold in Old Testament prophecy were inaugurated by Christ's resurrection (Acts 2:16–17). The time of waiting is over, and God is conducting the final phase of his victorious warfare against evil. By such reckoning, today is "the last hour" (1 John 2:18).

The wording in 1:1 seems to be built on Daniel 2:45, where God showed King Nebuchadnezzar "what will take place in the future." In Revelation 1:1, God shows his servants what must take place "soon." In Daniel, the vision is impressively far-ranging. It starts with Nebuchadnezzar's time, but then reaches out to encompass subsequent pagan world empires until the times when God's kingdom is established (Dan. 2:44–45). The kingdom of God was inaugurated by the first coming of Christ (Mark 1:15; Luke 11:20; Rom. 14:17), but its consummation is still to come. We live "in the last days" (2 Tim. 3:1, 12; Heb. 1:2), in the midst of fulfillments that are still working themselves out. Daniel spoke of events that, from his perspective, were in the distant future. These events are now occurring around us. Hence, Revelation properly says that they are "soon" to occur, in contrast to their distance from the time of Daniel. We are to understand that these days—from the first century until now—are the end times of spiritual conflict, in which "many antichrists" operate (1 John 2:18). Whether a clock measures the time until the Second Coming as a few hours or many centuries is irrelevant.

Verses 2 and 3 characterize Revelation in helpful ways. It is **the testimony of Jesus Christ** (v. 2). Because imminent persecution threatens to suppress Christian witness (17:6), Revelation is full of the theme of witness. Jesus Christ is the preeminent witness (1:5; 3:14; 19:11). Imitation of him may include martyrdom (12:11). Revelation itself is a witness, a testimony. It intends in turn to strengthen the testimony of its readers. Its message carries full divine authority and authenticity (22:20, 6, 16; 19:10).

Revelation not only pronounces judgment on the faithless, but blessing on the faithful (1:3; 14:13; 16:15; 19:9; 20:6; 22:7, 14). In verse 3, the blessing is specifically on those who read the book and on those who hear it. God encourages us not to shy away from it just because some have wrongly viewed it as an impossible puzzle. In the first century, **the one who reads** would refer to a person reading the book out loud to a Christian congregation. Reading out loud was especially important when few copies were available and when some people could not read. But it is still valuable today, because churches as a body, and not merely Christians as individuals, are to respond to it (1:11; 2:1–3:22).

In verse 3, Revelation is said to be **prophecy** (see also 22:7–10, 18–19). Like Old Testament prophecy, Revelation combines visions of the future with exhortation to faithfulness. Prophecy is a preeminent form of the witness that all of us are to give as Christians (see the note on 1:2).

We are to **take to heart** what is written (1:3). Revelation is not intended to tickle our fancy, but to strengthen our hearts (see "Schools of Interpretation" in the Introduction).

The Letter's Greeting (1:4–5a)

1:4–5a consists of a greeting that belongs to the opening part of a normal Greek letter (see "Structure" in the Introduction). In the first century, instead of the modern form "Dear Mary," people wrote "John to Mary" (author to reader), as the example in Acts 23:26 shows. Paul may have been the first to give letters a specifically Christian thrust by adding "grace to you and peace" instead of the more colorless introduction "greetings" (Acts 23:26; James 1:1).

The human author identifies himself simply as **John** (1:4). John the apostle was so well known to the seven churches that he did not need a more precise identification (see "Author and Date" in the Introduction).

The book is addressed **to the seven churches in the province of Asia** (cf. 1:11; 2:1–3:22). Revelation is organized in sevens (see "Structure" in the Introduction), seven being the symbolic number of completeness (Gen. 2:2–3). The choice of seven churches not only expresses this theme but hints at the wider relevance of the message to all churches in all times (cf. 1:1, 3; 2:7, 11, 17, 29; 3:6, 13, 22; 22:7, 11–14, 16, 18–21) (see "Occasion and Purpose" in the Introduction).

The Roman province of Asia was located in what is now western Turkey. The apostle John resided in Ephesus, in Asia Minor, before he was banished (1:9). He knew and sympathized with the people to whom he wrote. The incarnation of Christ is unique, but its principle is imitated every time God comes and speaks to us through human beings who are close to us and can identify with our circumstances.

Salvation comes **from him who is, and who was, and who is to come.** This designation of God is similar to the divine name in Exodus 3:14–15 (see also 1:8). God is the lord of the present, the past, and the future. Revelation deliberately introduces grammatical irregularities, which we can only begin to capture in English by translating "from he who is, and who was, and who is to come." Using an unchangeable *he*, instead of the expected *him*, underlines the absoluteness of God in his being, his sovereignty, and his relation to time. We might have expected the last of the three phrases to be "who will be." Instead, we have "who is to come," which underlines the dynamic unfolding of God's plan. The meaning of the future resides ultimately in the expectation that God will come. He will appear in a final manifestation that brings history to its consummation. Accordingly, the drama of Revelation moves toward the Second Coming and stirs up our anticipation and hope for the day of Christ's appearing. The King is coming!

What are **the seven spirits**? From God alone come grace and peace, so we cannot make this phrase refer to mere creatures. The phrase describes the Holy Spirit in sevenfold fullness (see 4:5; Zech. 4:2, 6). Grace and peace originate with the Trinity: God the Father ("him who is"), the Son (1:5), and the Spirit (cf. 1 Peter 1:1–2; 2 Cor. 13:14).

The key role of Jesus Christ in the whole of Revelation is already anticipated in verse 5a. Christ is **the faithful witness,** whom our witness imitates (see 1:2). He is **the firstborn from the dead,** meaning that his resurrection is the foundation and pattern for the promised resurrection of believers (see Col. 1:18). Christ was apparently defeated when his enemies succeeded in putting him to death. But this apparent defeat turned into a glorious, everlasting victory through his resurrection. Likewise, if Christians have to face martyrdom, their death is a defeat only in the eyes of the world. God will apply Christ's victory to those who die for him (2:10; 11:11–12, 18; 14:13; 20:4–6; see the note on 1:18). Finally, Christ is **the ruler of the kings of the earth.** Roman imperial power or modern state power may seem very impressive and terrifying, but Christ's power is infinitely greater. (On God's rule, see the note on 4:1–5:14 and "Schools of Interpretation" in the Introduction.)

Praise (1:5b–8)

John praises God in a way that is similar to the beginning of most Pauline letters. The themes of God's sovereignty, redemption, and the Second Coming recur throughout Revelation.

Christ has loved us and freed us (1:5b), as Revelation shows more fully in 5:1–14 and 19:1–22:5. His love and his conquest over sin give us security in the midst of the trials and disasters that Revelation will describe. And they give us motivation to persevere when persecution or temptation or weariness threatens to overwhelm us.

Freeing us from sin removes negative consequences. The positive side of redemption is found in being made **a kingdom and priests** (v. 6). Saints enjoy God's rule and, as priests, have intimate access to him (Heb. 10:19–22; 1 Peter 2:5–9). In the future, they will reign with him (2:26–27; 3:21; 5:10; 20:4, 6). Even now people from all nations share in the priestly privileges given to Israel in Exodus 19:6. The purposes of redemption that were embodied in the Exodus and the purposes of dominion that were given to man at creation are both fulfilled through Christ (Rev. 5:9–10).

The theme of priestly worship and access to God is complementary to the temple theme in Revelation (see the note on 4:1–5:14).

In response to God's salvation, praise and worship are fitting (v. 6). The theme of worship and praise of God extends throughout Revelation. Note the praises in 4:8, 11; 5:9–10, 12–13; 7:12; 11:15, 17–18; 12:10–12; 15:3–4; 19:1–8. Utterances of praise are an integral part of the spiritual war. True worship expresses our allegiance to God. This worship should then spill over with profound effect throughout our life.

As an integral aspect of our worship, we long for the second coming of Christ (1:7). Anticipation of this coming is important throughout Revelation. All persecution and opposition will cease, and Christian sufferers will be vindicated (21:4).

Worship depends on knowing who God is, and so he identifies himself as **the Alpha and the Omega.** Alpha is the first letter of the Greek alphabet, and omega is the last. God is the Alpha Creator and the Omega Consummator. He is Lord of all—past, present, and future (see 1:4; 4:1–5:14). His sovereignty in cre-

ation guarantees the fulfillment of his purposes in re-creation
(Rom. 8:18–25).

John's Commission (1:9–11)

In verses 9–11, an identification of John and his circumstances—in which he represents the whole church—prepares the
way for the first main vision in 1:12–3:22.

John could at this point have underlined his authority by calling himself an apostle or a prophet. Instead, he emphasizes his
solidarity with his readers: he is **your brother and compan-
ion.** He represents what all Christians can expect to go through.

Christian experience has two sides, **suffering and kingdom.**
Revelation, like the rest of the New Testament, is blunt about
the reality of suffering (e.g., Matt. 10:17–39; Acts 14:22; 2 Tim.
3:10–13; 1 Peter). But in suffering we have the consolation of
God's presence and his rule over us, which is already a participation in his kingdom (cf. 2 Cor. 1:3–11). In all circumstances
we are victorious (Rom. 8:28–39). The combination of suffering and kingdom calls for **patient endurance.** The exhortation
to endure and remain faithful runs through Revelation (2:2–3,
13, 19; 3:10; 6:11; 13:10; 14:12; 16:15; 18:4; 20:4; 22:7, 11, 14).
Revelation is not puzzling speculation, but practical exhortation
in the midst of persecution and temptation (see "Occasion and
Purpose" in the Introduction).

Patmos is a small island off the west coast of Asia Minor. It
had a Roman penal settlement, which was used for persons con-
sidered dangerous to good order. John had probably been exiled
there on account of his uncompromising loyalty to Christ. John
is thus a picture of the persecution that may come to any
Christian.

John received his revelations on **the Lord's Day,** Sunday, the
Christian day of worship in celebration of Christ's resurrection.
The Sunday celebration anticipates the celebration of God's fi-
nal victory (19:1–10).

John was **in the Spirit,** so that the Spirit gave him the visions and transported him to the vantage points for viewing them (see 4:2, 17:3; 21:10). The Spirit gave John inspired authority of a unique kind. But this unique level of inspiration is still a pattern for the witness that all Christians are to bear. The whole church is to "prophesy" in an extended sense, by bearing the "testimony of Jesus" (cf. 11:1–12; 12:17; 19:10; 22:9).

John heard **a loud voice** (v. 10). We infer from the subsequent verses that Christ is speaking. Elsewhere, loud voices and noises indicate the power and universal relevance of the messages and events (1:15; 4:1, 5; 5:2, 12; 6:1; 7:2, 10; 8:5, 13; 10:3; 11:12, 15, 19; 12:10; 14:7, 9, 15, 18; 19:1, 3, 6, 17). Sometimes angels, rather than Christ, are the speakers. But Christ always stands behind the angels as the ultimate mediator, whom they imitate. Only through Christ do we have access to God's plan, his will, and the visions of his glory.

The seven churches are named for the first time in verse 11 (see 1:4). They are listed in the order in which they will later receive distinct messages adapted to their needs (chapters 2–3). Perhaps intentionally, the order is also the one that would have been the most convenient for a messenger to deliver the book to the churches (fig. 14).

Vision of Christ (1:12–20)

In the first vision given to John, Christ appears to John in overwhelming glory (cf. 21:22–24). The description combines features from several places in the Old Testament (fig. 15). The phrase "like a son of man" (v. 13) alludes to Daniel 7:13. The features of verses 12–16 are reminiscent of Daniel 7:9–10; 10:5–6 and Ezekiel 1:25–28, but include more distant similarities to many Old Testament appearances of God. The vision shows Christ as judge and ruler—first of all over the churches (1:20–3:22), but also over the whole universe (1:17–18; 2:27; 3:21). His deity, his authority, and his conquest of death guarantee final victory (1:17–18; 17:14; 19:11–16). This vision of

FIG. 14. THE SEVEN CHURCHES

God's sovereignty, exercised through Christ, is a focal point in Revelation (see "Schools of Interpretation" in the Introduction). Christ's warriorlike fierceness and armorlike bronze (1:15) anticipate his role in the final battle (19:11–21) and recall God's battles in the Old Testament (Ex. 15:3; Deut. 32:41–42; Isa. 59:17–18; Zech. 14:3).

The lampstands symbolize the churches in their light-bearing or witness-bearing function (v. 20; cf. Matt. 5:14–16). The churches are the reality to which the symbolic lampstands in the tabernacle and the temple pointed forward.

Christ walks among the churches as Lord and Shepherd, just as God's cloud of glory condescended to dwell in the tabernacle and the temple, which had their lampstands (Ex. 25:31–40; 1 Kings 7:49). God's character as light (1 John 1:5) is supremely

FIG. 15. SIMILARITIES TO OLD TESTAMENT APPEARANCES OF GOD

Revelation 1:12–16	Ezekiel 1:25–28	Daniel 10:5–6	Daniel 7:9–10	Daniel 7:13–14
son of man	like that of a man	a man		son of man
robe		linen robe		
gold sash		gold sash		
white hair			white hair	
eyes like fire	fire	eyes like flame	fire	
feet like bronze	glowing metal	gleaming bronze		
voice like rushing water	sound like rushing water	sound of a multitude		
stars in hand				
face like the sun	radiance	like lightning		

manifested in Christ (John 1:4–5; 8:12; 9:5; Acts 26:13), but is also reflected in various ways in his creation: in fiery angels (Rev. 10:1; Ezek. 1:13; Dan. 10:5–6?), in natural light (Rev. 21:23; Gen. 1:3), in the temple lampstands, in the churches, and in individuals (Matt. 5:14–16). Christ thus presents the pattern in which the destiny of the whole universe is summed up (Eph. 1:10; Col. 1:16–17). Because all things hold together in Christ (Col. 1:17), the Trinitarian imagery of 1:12–20 and 4:1–5:14 forms a foundation in subtle ways for the whole of Revelation. Because the Trinity is deeply mysterious, the imagery of Revelation has inexhaustible profundity.

Now let us look at some of the details. Christ is described as **someone "like a son of man"** because he fulfills the vision of Daniel 7:13–14. Daniel sees in the distant future a mysterious, exalted human figure who brings to an end the succession of pagan, world-dominating kingdoms: Babylon, Medo-Persia, Greece, and Rome. What was distant for Daniel has now become reality through Christ's death and resurrection (verse 18). Christ has received the promised dominion from the Ancient of Days. The effects of his authority are still being worked out in history.

With the justice and discrimination of a judge, he weighs the good and the bad among the seven churches, and promises suitable rewards and punishments (chapters 2–3). He has the key role in judgment, not only for the churches, but also for the world at large (6:1; 19:11–21).

The special term used for Christ's long **robe** probably suggests a priestly robe, underlining his purity. Purity is required of churches and Christians if they are to remain in his presence (1:13, 20; 2:5). Purity is the foundation for the rectitude of his judgments. As priest, he takes care of the lampstands in God's temple.

The **sash** (a normal piece of men's clothing) corresponds to Daniel 10:5 and to the sash or waistband of the high priest (Ex. 28:8). What is striking is that it is **golden,** signifying the beauty, wealth, and exalted status of the one who wears it. The wealth of human beings is only a puny reflection of the majesty of God.

Christ's white head and hair correspond to the white of the Ancient of Days in Daniel 7:9, suggesting both purity and the wisdom associated with old age. Note that Christ shares the attributes of the Father, who is the reference point in Daniel 7:9–10.

His eyes blaze with **fire,** as in Daniel 10:6. Fire accompanies the appearance of God (theophany) in many cases in the Old Testament (e.g., Dan. 7:9; Ezek. 1:4, 13, 27; Ex. 19:18; 3:2; Gen. 15:17). His eyes can see the secrets of human hearts (Rev. 2:18, 23; Heb. 4:12–13) and burn away sin and impurity.

His feet were like bronze glowing in a furnace. The purifying power of the fiery eyes carries over its associations to the feet, which have a fiery glow. Similarly in the Old Testament, bright metal appears in the presence of God, as in Ezekiel 1:4, 7, 27 and Daniel 10:6. There seem to be a multiplicity of vague allusions here. Bronze is a harder and more ordinary metal than gold or silver, and was frequently used in weapons. This suggests an association with judgment and war. The brightness and the association with fire again suggest judgment, but accompanied by intense purity, beauty, and glory. See also 2:18.

The picture of Christ achieves its effect, not by limiting itself to some specific attribute of God, but by suggesting connections to many attributes, and by showing Christ as the original of which earthly splendors and earthly judges are only pale imitations.

Christ's voice sounded like **the sound of rushing waters.** This repeats the theme of loud, authoritative voices from God, as in 1:10. Loud sounds occur in Daniel 10:6, Ezekiel 1:24, and Exodus 19:16, 19.

In Christ's **right hand** were **seven stars,** signifying **the angels of the seven churches** (1:20). He has control over the whole heavenly host, of which these angels are a representative sample.

A **sword** (v. 16) comes out of his mouth. It signifies the swordlike capability of Christ's powerful word to bring punishment or reward (see Rev. 19:15, 21; Heb. 4:12–13; John 12:47–50; Matt. 7:24–27; Isa. 11:4).

His face was like the sun, continuing to emphasize the brilliant majesty of Christ's appearance. This theme appears in Revelation 10:1; 21:22–25, Isaiah 60:1–3, 19–20, and Ezekiel 1:27.

John falls down, overwhelmed (v. 17). Christ is our friend, according to John 15:14–15. But he is more than a mere friend: he is awesome in majesty, power, and purity. Too many Christians in our generation have seen Christ only as a "buddy," losing sight of his majesty. Revelation provides a strong correction to this notion. C. S. Lewis captures something of this picture in a famous passage from *The Lion, the Witch, and the Wardrobe,* in which a lion represents the Christ figure:

> "Aslan a man!" said Mr Beaver sternly. "Certainly not. I tell you he is the King of the wood and the son of the great Emperor-beyond-the-sea. Don't you know who is the King of Beasts? Aslan is a lion—the Lion, the great Lion."
>
> "Ooh!" said Susan, "I'd thought he was a man. Is he—quite safe? I shall feel rather nervous about meeting a lion."

"That you will, dearie, and no mistake," said Mrs Beaver; "if there's anyone who can appear before Aslan without their knees knocking, they're either braver than most or else just silly."

"Then he isn't safe?" said Lucy.

"Safe?" said Mr Beaver; "don't you hear what Mrs Beaver tells you? Who said anything about safe? 'Course he isn't safe. But he's good. He's the King, I tell you."

"I'm longing to see him," said Peter, "even if I do feel frightened when it comes to the point."

"That's right, son of Adam," said Mr Beaver, bringing his paw down on the table with a crash that made all the cups and saucers rattle. "And so you shall. Word has been sent that you are to meet him, to-morrow if you can, at the Stone Table."[17]

Christ says to John, "Do not be afraid" (v. 17), and he says the same thing to us throughout Revelation: "Whatever may happen to you, I am who I am, and I have the victory."

Christ is **the First and the Last,** Lord over the beginning and the end, just as is God the Father (Rev. 22:13; 1:8; Isa. 41:4; 44:6; 48:12). He is also Lord over the middle point, in that his death and resurrection, as a middle point, have turned back the power of death, not only for himself, but for all those people who belong to him. His possession of the keys of death (v. 18) anticipates 20:14 and 21:4. At the consummation, death shall be no more. The triumph through this one man then extends in its perfection to us, so that it becomes the permanent triumph of the entire new world (2:8; 5:9–10; 20:4–5; 22:1). Analogously, because of his transcendent authority, Christ is able to give the church the promise of victory over death and Hades (Matt. 16:18–19; see Rev. 3:7).

Verse 19 suggests a threefold division of Revelation into past (**what you have seen:** 1:12–16), present (**what is now:** 2:1–3:22), and future (**what will take place later:** 4:1–22:5). Note the similar wording in 1:19 and 4:1. But the division is only a rough one, since each portion of the book contains some references to all three periods.

The Messages
to the Seven Churches (2:1–3:22)

In Revelation 2–3 Christ shows care for the churches by addressing each one according to its needs, with encouragement, rebuke, exhortation, and promise. He shows detailed knowledge of their condition ("I know"). Each message contains allusions to circumstances or traditions of the city, some of which we are doubtless still unaware of. At the same time, all the churches are caught up in a universal calling to faithfulness and endurance until the promises reach their fulfillment in the heavenly Jerusalem. Their struggles contrast with the peace and satisfaction pictured in 21:1–22:5. The exhortations are reinforced in all but one case (Laodicea) by an opening allusion to some element of the majestic vision of 1:12–20. The exhortations therefore have universal relevance.

Moreover, the churches mentioned in Revelation 2–3 number exactly seven, the number that symbolizes completeness. They stand for all the churches of that time and ours. In fact, the triumphs, failures, and struggles of these churches are a kind of miniature catalogue of the sorts of things that we can expect to find in other churches throughout history. (Some interpreters have assigned the seven churches to seven successive ages of church history, a procedure for which Revelation gives no warrant.) According to God's point of view, not all churches are equally healthy. Their faithfulness or laziness or complacency or tolerance of false doctrine is important to him, and makes a dif-

ference both in how they should respond and how they are
judged. We likewise need Christlike discernment, illumined by
the Spirit and by these examples, if we are to evaluate our own
church situation accurately and respond faithfully.

Each message has the same basic form:

1. Address: "To the angel of the church in . . . write."
2. Identification of Christ, alluding back to his majesty displayed in 1:12–20: "These are the words of . . ."
3. Claim of knowledge: "I know . . ."
4. Evaluation: rebukes and/or commendations.
5. Promise or threat: usually "I will . . ."
6. Promise to "him who overcomes."
7. "He who has an ear, let him hear what the Spirit says to the
   churches."

Elements 6 and 7 can occur in reverse order, and element 5 can
be mixed in with element 4.

Each message in also distinctive, corresponding to the distinctive character and circumstances of the particular church addressed. We may summarize the differences in figure 16.

FIG. 16. DISTINCTIVE FEATURES OF THE SEVEN CHURCHES

Church	Character of Christ	Strength	Problem	Duty	Promise
Ephesus	authority	doctrinal zeal	lost love	repent	tree of life
Smyrna	giving life	spiritually rich		suffer for Christ	freedom from death
Pergamum	warrior against sin	holding fast	false teaching	repent	spiritual significance
Thyatira	searching heart	love, service	false teaching, immorality (Jezebel)	repudiate Jezebel	rule over nations
Sardis	source of Spirit	a few faithful saints	spiritually dead	awake!	white robe (honor)
Philadelphia	opening door	keeping the word	little strength	continue	secure dwelling
Laodicea	true witness		worthless	admit need; receive from Christ	fellowship

Who are the "angels" of the churches? The underlying Greek word can mean simply "messenger." So some people have seen here a reference to the messengers who physically delivered the document to the churches. Others have seen a reference to the pastors of the churches, in their capacity as message bearers of God. But the visionary context of the book of Revelation suggests that actual angels are in view. Specific angels have evidently been given responsibility with respect to specific churches, in a manner analogous to the attachment of heavenly "princes" to specific nations in Daniel 10:12–11:1. God's heavenly presence is the power center for the entire universe. The heavenly and earthly realms therefore interlock, and situations and processes in heaven have correspondences in mysterious fashion to processes on earth. Thus, the same messages go both to heavenly angels and to corresponding churches on earth.

The Message to Ephesus (2:1–7)

The church in Ephesus receives a mixed evaluation. It has commendable zeal for sound doctrine and the rejection of false doctrine (vv. 2, 6). But, like many a modern student focused on doctrine, it is short on love. The godly response is to see the failing and repent.

Otherwise, Christ threatens to **remove your lampstand** (v. 5). He alludes to the fact that the city of Ephesus had to change location because of the gradual silting up of its river, the Caÿster. It had been "removed" from earlier locations. By analogy, Christ threatens to dislocate and restructure the church unless she repents.

Who are the **Nicolaitans**? We know of them only from this passage and later commentaries. They were a heretical group, probably holding views similar to the teaching of "Balaam" and "Jezebel" (see 2:14–15, 20). Christ **hates** their practices (v. 6). Their deeds are immoral and impure, in contrast to the purity of Christ, and this contrast makes them bad enough. But by teaching and enticing others, the Nicolaitans spread soul-threatening contagion and spiritual disaster to others as well. Likewise in our day, we need to take seriously the threat of false doctrine and evil practices.

Christ addresses **him who overcomes** in this and parallel statements to the other churches. He promises to faithful saints participation in all aspects of the new Jerusalem that is to appear (2:7, 11, 17, 26; 3:5, 12, 21; cf. 21:1–22:5). The **tree of life,** which appears in 22:2, symbolizes eternal, abundant life in the presence of God (see John 10:10; 14:6; 4:14; 5:40).

The Message to Smyrna (2:8–11)

Smyrna is one of two churches for whom Christ gives encouragement and not rebuke. Smyrna faced serious persecution, including even death (v. 10). Christ's assurance begins with underlining the fact that he is victorious over death (v. 8).

Non-Christian Jews may have been trying to get Christians in trouble by claiming that the church was not another Jewish sect, but an essentially non-Jewish group. If so, in the eyes of the Roman government they could, like all Gentiles, be required to show political loyalty to the government by participating in emperor worship. If they refused, as Christians must, they could be executed for treason. (See "Author and Date" in the Introduction.)

Such a situation would explain the phrase **synagogue of Satan.** The Jewish synagogue in Smyrna was not composed of all Jews in the area, nor of people who had never heard of Jesus Christ, but specifically of Jews who rejected the gospel. (Doubtless some Jews had responded favorably to the gospel and joined the church.) The Jews who rejected Jesus professed to worship God, but their opposition to Christ showed that they were in fact under the control of satanic darkness (2 Cor. 4:4). Behind human opposition stands the more fundamental opposition of Satan, who seeks by all means to destroy the church (Rev. 12:13–13:1).

Like others under persecution, the Smyrnans must persevere—they must **be faithful** (v. 10). The city of Smyrna prided itself on faithfulness to Rome. But the only loyalty that ultimately matters is loyalty to Christ.

Christ promises **the crown of life.** The thematic connections here go in several directions. Christ himself, as the one risen from the dead (v. 8; 1:18), is the ultimate source of true life, life from the dead. The promise also answers deftly the threat of persecution leading to death. In addition, Christ links his claims with the life of the city as a whole. Smyrna's goddess Cybele is pictured in coins with a crown consisting of a city battlement. The Smyrnan buildings on Mt. Pagos were said to look like a crown. Over against these claims, Jesus offers to impart the true crown.

The Message to Pergamum (2:12–17)

The church in Pergamum has borne persecution well (v. 13), but fails to reject false teachers (vv. 14–15). They must take up the fight for truth, imitating Christ's zeal for truth (v. 16).

Christ describes their location as **where Satan has his throne.** Pergamum possessed the oldest temple in Asia Minor devoted to emperor worship. But other, subtler satanic influences were present, as we learn from the mention of Balaam and the Nicolaitans (cf. 2:6). Balaam (Num. 22:5) gave Balak advice leading to the incident in Numbers 25:1–4, where Israel went astray after false gods and practiced sexual immorality. Similarly, Jezebel (Rev. 2:20) and other professing Christians in the seven churches were indulging in pleasures offered by their pagan environment (see 17:1–19:10). The Nicolaitans, the same group as in 2:6, were probably a heretical group with teaching similar to what Balaam represented.

Christ's promises to the faithful again contain multiple allusions. The **hidden manna** (v. 17) perhaps alludes to the manna kept preserved in the Most Holy Place of the tabernacle (Ex. 16:33–35; Heb. 9:4). Christ promises to nourish the faithful with an unfailing supply of heavenly, spiritual food (see John 6:32–58). He also promises **a white stone,** recalling all the references in Revelation to white as a symbol for purity (e.g., 7:13; 19:14). Interestingly, pink granite dominated the buildings in Pergamum, because it was available locally. But in the ruins there, one also finds special inscription stones of white marble, which would have had to be imported. These white stones gained in value, not only from their superior beauty, but from the difficulty of acquiring them. Over against the prestige attaching to earthly displays, Christ promises the only prestige that matters— to be known by God. He thus gives a fitting motive to people who are in danger of being seduced into illicit mixing with paganism and its pleasures.

The Message to Thyatira (2:18–29)

The church at Thyatira has the opposite problem from the one in Ephesus. Love is strong here (v. 19), but not doctrinal purity (vv. 20–23).

As usual, Christ singles out those characteristics of his that are most relevant to the church's situation. The Son of God has eyes **like blazing fire** to search the heart (v. 23) and feet of power to trample the wicked (cf. Isa. 63:3, 6). The feet are **like burnished bronze.** This is linked to 1:15, and from there to Old Testament appearances of God that have bright metallic luster (Ezek. 1:4, 7, 27; Dan. 10:6). There is also a suggestive link with the circumstances of the city. Thyatira had a guild of bronze workers who were famous throughout the region, and doubtless the whole city prided itself on its unique bronze products. Moreover, the Greek word for **burnished bronze** in v. 18 is unique: it occurs only here, in 1:15, and in later commentaries, but nowhere else in all of Greek literature! It may well have been the trade name for the special kind of bronze produced in Thyatira. The Thyatiran guild carefully guarded a secret process for making this prized kind of bronze, so that no one could get it except from Thyatira—no one, that is, except Christ. In him are hidden all the treasures of wisdom and knowledge (Col. 2:3). Thyatiran secrets about bronze are only a tiny echo of his wisdom and uniqueness. We have here an indirect rebuke of those who lust after secret knowledge, apart from Christ (v. 24).

The leader of the deviant group in the church at Thyatira is a woman called "Jezebel," after the Jezebel of 1 Kings 16:31; 19:1–2; 21:5–26; 2 Kings 9:30–37. Like the Old Testament Jezebel, this woman seduced people into sexual immorality and idolatry, two major forms of indulgence in pagan Asia Minor. See Rev. 14:8 and 17:1–19:10. She may have argued that those with her secret knowledge (v. 24) could see that an idol is nothing (cf. 1 Cor. 10:19), and that for people with deep "spiritual" knowledge, the use of the body no longer made a difference. Her message was welcome because it made it much easier to mix with pagans in business and in social affairs, where food dedicated to idols and prostitution might be present. Sin can always come up with excuses to do what it wants, to do what is convenient and comfortable. It may take a prophetically penetrating criticism like John's to bring people up short. Or it may take even more: the hand of God in punishment (vv. 22–23). Although it may be painful, this punishment is for the good of God's children (Heb. 12:5–13).

Christ promises **authority over the nations** (v. 26) to people who must have felt puny and powerless in worldly ways. They did not enjoy the fame of Thyatiran bronze workers, or privileged access to secrets of worldly power, or smooth social relations with pagan idolaters. But they will inherit a much superior privilege. They will **dash** the nations **to pieces.** This is not wanton destruction, but fulfillment of the plan of God set forth in Psalm 2:9. Specifically, the rebellion of nations against Christ receives God's wrath and destruction. All rebellion is forcibly wiped out. Christians now know that the destruction of rebellion takes two very different forms: repentance and faith in Christ lead to crucifying the old rebellion of Christians, whereas the fire of hell ends the rebellion of the unrepentant.

Christ promises **the morning star** (v. 28) to the victors. Elsewhere he is himself the Morning Star (22:16). The brightness of a star suggests connections with the promise that churches and Christians will show forth light that reflects the original light of Christ (1:13, 16). The morning star, Venus, is the brightest starlike object in the night sky. The prominence of the morning star also suggests an answer to the unimportance of Christians in the world: they have weight and significance through Christ, and in the coming age their status will be made manifest.

The Message to Sardis (3:1–6)

The churches in Sardis and Laodicea receive the most severe rebukes. Sardis is dead, though still with a chance of reviving life (v. 2). And a few at Sardis remain faithful (v. 4). But the situation is all the more dangerous because the Christians at Sardis are deluded about their true state (v. 1). They are unconcerned. This lesson is devastatingly relevant for us. Groups can bear the name of church, and have a certain reputation, when it is doubtful that they are truly churches at all. The essence of a church is not its programs, buildings, past achievements, reputation, institutional greatness, or formal doctrinal correctness, but its spiritual life. This life comes only through fellowship with the living Christ, and is demonstrated through the seriousness of repentance and obedience. Christ reminds the people at Sardis that he has **the seven spirits of God.** Only through the Holy Spirit, represented by the figure of seven spirits (1:4), do we receive life in God.

The church at Sardis once did have life (v. 3). Spiritual decline is a real possibility, then and now.

Christ calls first for repentance. But in his zeal he is prepared to take stronger measures if repentance is not forthcoming. **I will come like a thief** (v. 3). The seemingly impregnable fortress of Sardis had in wartime been captured twice by surprise, probably at night. Christ warns that a similar experience will befall the church, unless they wake up.

Promises of purity, vindication, and reward come first of all to the "few" at Sardis who remain faithful (v. 4). But these few become an incentive to others to regain their lost spirituality. Essentially the same promise is given to everyone **who overcomes** (v. 5). Life returns in fullness, as is fittingly symbolized by **the book of life,** the heavenly roster of those destined to receive new life (see 13:8; 17:8; John 6:39).

The Message to Philadelphia (3:7–13)

Philadelphia, like Smyrna, receives commendation. They have only **little strength,** but they have **kept my word** (v. 8). Like the church in Smyrna (2:9), they are being opposed by non-Christian Jews (v. 9). Christ holds out promises of victory and security to encourage them to persevere.

Christ **holds the key of David** (v. 7), representing the power of opening and shutting, analogous to the keys of death and Hades in 1:18. Christ's authority is a surpassing fulfillment of the "key of David" prophecy in Isaiah 22:20–25. What neither Eliakim nor any other saint of the Old Testament could do, Christ has done. His reliability and strength are such that one can rest on him all the weight of the host of redeemed people and their destiny.

The key that Christ holds represents his authority to set before Philadelphia **an open door** (v. 8). Since a road led from Philadelphia into the interior of Asia Minor, Christ may be saying that he is opening a way for the church to evangelize the interior. However, nothing else in the context suggests a focus on evangelism. More likely, then, the open door symbolizes freedom to approach God himself (cf. 4:1). As a result of this privilege, the church has freedom to grow and develop spiritually, in spite of the opposition of Jews and the threat of trial (v. 10).

As in 2:9, the synagogue of non-Christian Jews is called a **synagogue of Satan,** not only because they were rejecting the truth of Christ, but because they actively opposed and hindered the church (see on 2:9).

The "little strength" of the Philadelphian church tempted it to feel insecure and terrified. Christ promises security in a variety of ways. First, in response to their fear of trial, he promises to keep them from **the hour of trial that is going to come . . .** (v. 10). This most likely refers to the various trials and punishments that God sends in later chapters (6–11; 16–18; 19:11–21). These trials come on **those who live on the earth.** Here, as elsewhere in Revelation, these are not all the inhabitants of earth, but those who are worldly in spirit (6:10; 8:13; 11:10; 13:8, 12, 14; 17:2). We might say that their citizenship is on the earth, as opposed to Christians with citizenship in heaven (Phil. 3:20; Heb. 12:22–24). God knows Christians as his own, seals them, and protects them (Rev. 9:4). We are not immune from the normal ups and downs of life (Phil. 4:11–13), nor from persecution (Rev. 2:10, 13; 2 Tim. 3:12–13; Acts 14:22; 1 Thess. 3:3–5). But we are protected as children in the Father's hand (cf. Rom. 8:28–39; John 10:27–30).

Second, Christ promises to make the saints in Philadelphia **a pillar in the temple.** Since Philadelphia had suffered from earthquakes, people were afraid to live any longer within the old city limits and were building houses in the surrounding area. The insecurity of the city as a whole made the promise of security and stability particularly pointed.

Third, Christ promises to write the name of God on the faithful (v. 12). The name of God is not only a sign of intimacy, of being a member of his family, but here in Revelation a sign of ownership and protection, as we see in 14:1 compared to 13:16. It is equivalent to the seal on the forehead in 9:4 and 7:1–8 (cf. Hag. 2:23; Mal. 3:17–18; Ezek. 9:4–11; Ex. 28:36; 19:5–6).

The Message to Laodicea (3:14–22)

The church at Laodicea receives no commendations, but only rebukes. Their fundamental problem is complacency, self-satisfaction, and self-reliance. They *think* that they are rich and well-supplied in everything (v. 17). Ironically, this claim exposes them to greater danger and poverty, because they have no sense of their need to admit powerlessness and helplessness, to turn to Christ, and to receive from him true riches and healing. Christ shocks them into reality by declaring that their real state is the opposite of what they pridefully thought.

Christ reinforces his evaluation by reminding them of the reliability of his words. As **the faithful and true witness** (v. 14), his word is more accurate and telling than their complacent self-evaluation. Christ describes himself as **the Amen,** using the Hebrew word translated "truly" or "verily" in Jesus' common saying, "Truly, truly, I say to you." (The NIV typically translates this as "I tell you the truth.") He is the Truth, as in John 14:6. Hence, he tells the painful and unpleasant truth to the Laodiceans.

Christ is also **the beginning of God's creation.** Some translations (such as the NIV) read, "the ruler of God's creation." But this is a less likely meaning. The thought is similar to 1:5, where Christ is "the firstborn from the dead" (see Col. 1:18). By his resurrection, he has inaugurated or begun the *new* creation.[18] Only in and through him will the Laodiceans receive spiritual renewal now, and the resurrection of the body when the new heaven and the new earth come.

Christ begins his evaluation of the Laodiceans by saying that they are **neither cold nor hot.** Laodicea's water supply had to be provided from a distant source through pipes. The resulting water was lukewarm and barely drinkable. By contrast, the neighboring town of Hierapolis had medicinal hot springs, and neighboring Colossae was supplied by a cold mountain stream. Christ urges the church to be refreshing (cold) or medicinally healing (hot), rather than like the Laodicean water supply. Be able to minister in some valuable way, rather than being worthless, as lukewarm water is! His message must have been particularly meaningful and piercing to the Laodiceans, because, proud as they were of their supposed riches and self-sufficiency, they daily experienced the disgusting and inferior quality of their water, in contrast to the water of the neighboring cities. Laodiceans felt like spitting out their water, and so Christ uses the same stunning image of spitting to express the worthlessness of their complacency.

Moreover, the problems of the church in Laodicea echoed the problems associated with the whole city. The entire city prided itself on its self-sufficiency. After earthquakes caused considerable damage in Laodicea, the Roman authorities in the region were willing to help with repair and restoration. But Laodicea refused the help and boasted that it had recovered entirely through its own resources and ability.

In response to the Laodiceans' need, Christ promises gold, white clothes, and salve. The gold clearly comes from Christ's own transcendent resources, as we are reminded by the gold and the refining fire in 1:13, 15. It answers the Laodicean boast of being rich in itself. The white clothes link up ironically to another local pride: Laodicea was well known throughout the region as a source of black wool. Moreover, the city was also famous for its guild of physicians. Certain references to ways of healing the eyes seem to suggest that this guild of physicians may have produced a special eye salve claiming to have healing properties. Like the special bronze from Thyatira, the eye salve from Laodicea would have been the pride of the city. But who really has the healing powers that matter? Once again, Christ, as Lord of all creation and Redeemer of the world, has the healing of which any earthly healing is only a poor shadow.

Christ's message, so antithetical to what the Laodiceans expected, would have been hard to swallow. So he affectionately reminds them that love motivates his rebuke (v. 19). He desires not to alienate or offend them, but to bring them to repentance, so that they may have fellowship with him (v. 20). He is eager to extend that fellowship, and all the glorious riches and healing that come with it, if only they will hear his voice and admit their need. He promises to eat with them, alluding to the fellowship with Christ expressed in the Lord's Supper (Luke 22:19; 1 Cor. 11:17–34). In the Lord's Supper, the Lord comes and feeds us with himself, as indeed he does through the fellowship that we have throughout our life (John 6:25–59). Revelation 3:20 has often been used as an evangelistic text, but in its original context it is a promise directed at complacent Christians, who need to confess their dependence and restore fellowship with the Master.

God's Throne Room (4:1–5:14)

I n Revelation 4–5 God appears in a beautiful scene of worship as the magnificent king of heaven and earth. He is surrounded by angelic courtiers (cf. 1 Kings 22:19; Job 1:6; 2:1; Ps. 89:6–7; Ezek. 1; Dan. 7:9–10). His rule was established in creation (4:11), is exercised in the entire panorama of history (6:1–22:5), is consummated through the Lamb (5:1–14; 22:1), and is celebrated in songs of praise (see on 1:6). Revelation is preeminently a book about God and his greatness. The secrets of history and of spiritual conflict center on God himself. The whole universe is destined to be filled with his glory (21:22–23), his goodness (22:1–5), and his praise (5:13). Hence, the course of all history is revealed in miniature here (cf. Matt. 6:10). (See "Schools of Interpretation" in the Introduction.)

When God's people are beset by temptation or persecution, a revelation of God's character and glory is the best remedy. His power guarantees the final victory, his justice guarantees vindication of the right, and his goodness and magnificence guarantee blessing and comfort. The blood of the Lamb demonstrates that solid redemption has already been accomplished. Even in the midst of trials and persecutions, God is still the ruler. He controls everything.

John's vision is a little like a visit to an airport control tower. At a busy airport, a casual observer looking out the windows sees planes, vehicles, and baggage going every which way. But if the observer is escorted up to the control tower, he can see the over-

all plan of the airport and hear the directives going out to execute the plans of the controllers. Suddenly the goings-on down
below make sense. So it is with John. Through his vision, we are
transported into the "control tower" for the entire universe.
From this vantage point, as we understand the Controller and
his plans, things fall into place. And even if they sometimes escape our comprehension, we know the One who does comprehend it all. His plans cannot and will not fail!

In the Old Testament, the tabernacle (Ex. 25–40) and the
temple (1 Kings 5–7; 2 Chron. 2–4) were images or shadows of
God's throne room in heaven (Ex. 25:40; Heb. 8:5–6; 9:1–14).
John sees the heavenly original rather than an earthly copy.
Revelation thus fittingly contains many allusions to the temple
(3:12; 7:15; 11:19; 14:15, 17; 15:5–16:1; 16:17; 21:22) and to
elements within it: for example, the lamps (4:5; cf. 1:12), the living creatures like cherubim (4:6–9), incense and prayer (5:8),
songs of praise like those offered by the Levitical singers in the
Old Testament (4:8, 11; 5:9–13; 1 Chron. 16), a sacrifice (5:6,
9), the ark of the covenant (11:19), the altar (11:1), and the
outer court (11:2).

The tabernacle and the temple in the Old Testament were
centers for worship. In this respect also they were images of
God's presence in heaven. The history of the universe, from creation to consummation, finds its significance in worship. God is
glorious. Those who know and see him cannot but stand in awe
of him, and worship him with profound gratitude, joy, and satisfaction. "You will fill me with joy in your presence, with eternal
pleasures at your right hand" (Ps. 16:11). Because God is who
he is, he is not only the creator of earthly pleasures, but the very
fountainhead of all joy. Creatures find their consummate fulfillment, the meaning and full satisfaction of their existence, in worshiping, serving, and adoring him. God created the heavens and
the earth, and everything he made was "very good" (Gen. 1:31).
It was very good because it reflected and displayed something
of the glory of its maker (cf. Isa. 6:3). But the consummation

will display his glory in a yet fuller and incomprehensibly richer fashion (Rev. 21:23). God's victory will surpass all expectations (Eph. 3:20); we now grasp it only dimly (1 Cor. 13:9–12). Thus, theologically and biblically speaking, the throne room of God in Revelation 4 represents the heart of the universe, the heart of meaning, the heart of history. Our lives are renewed through worship, through adoring the God who created us and saw fit to redeem us through the blood of the Lamb. Revelation renews us, not so much by telling us about particular future events, as by showing us God, who will bring all events to pass in his own time and his own way.

God and His Angelic Court (4:1–11)

A door stands open in heaven to give John access to it and to the vision that he will see. A voice invites him up, the same voice as in 1:10, the voice of Christ. It is always through Christ alone that we have access to God, and the same is true for John. **Come up here** indicates that John ascends into heaven, whether in the body or out of it (2 Cor. 12:2–3). Similarly, Moses went up to Mount Sinai (Ex. 19:3, 20), and Paul was caught up to heaven (2 Cor. 12:2) to receive special revelations. Ezekiel saw heaven opened (Ezek. 1:1), as did John. Although John's experience was unique, God gives us a description of what John saw. He thus gives the whole church of God access to the heavenly sphere. Through the pages of Revelation, then, we can share in the benefits of John's experience.

The content of John's vision concerns what **must take place after this.** This language is similar to that in 1:19; it refers to the whole of 4:1–22:5. Because God is in control and has fore-ordained the entire course of history (Eph. 1:11; Isa. 46:10), he can tell beforehand the character of the entire age leading up to the Second Coming. This guarantee from God is reassuring to believers who must face hardship, persecution, or even death.

John is **in the Spirit** (v. 2). As in 1:10, 17:3, and 21:10, the Spirit brings him to the location from which he will see the vision. And, more broadly, the Spirit supervises and controls the entire visionary process (cf., e.g., Ezek. 2:2). The Spirit is the mediator of all prophetic revelations and the mediator of our understanding of spiritual things as well (1 Cor. 2:9–16).

At the center of the vision is God's throne in heaven, representing his kingly rule. God's sovereignty is a fundamental theme throughout Revelation. As the vision unfolds, we find that God is surrounded by successive circles of servants: four living creatures, twenty-four elders, and myriads of angels (5:11). God is the all-important, all-determining spiritual center and power center for the universe.

Someone sits on the throne. But the details of God's appearance are not described, reminding us that his greatness always exceeds our grasp (see 1:12–20).

What is the meaning of the jasper, the carnelian, and the rainbow resembling an emerald? It is important to keep in mind the big picture. God's appearance far surpasses the splendor of any earthly king's court. The precious stones display his wealth, his beauty, and his glory. "God is light; in him there is no darkness at all" (1 John 1:5). Fittingly, his throne displays beautiful, multicolored light. The jasper is white or translucent (21:11). Carnelian is red, and emerald is green. One is reminded of the bejeweled splendor of the new Jerusalem (21:11, 19–20), the high priest's breastpiece (Ex. 28:17–20), and some Old Testament theophanies (Ex. 24:10; Ezek. 1:16, 22, 26, 28). In ancient times, it was not easy for an earthly king to obtain precious stones except through international trade (cf. Ezek. 28:13, concerning the international trading city of Tyre). Hence, the presence of these precious stones indirectly underlines the international reach of God's kingship.

God is himself the ultimate source of splendor and beauty. His splendor is partly reflected in the things that he has made: the brightness and colors of the sun, of heavenly bodies, of the rainbow, and of precious jewels (cf. Isa. 6:3). The church and its members are in turn to reflect his splendor through the holiness of their lives (Rev. 21:19–20; 19:8; 22:11; Matt. 5:14–16; 1 Peter 3:3–5).

We may discern a general pattern in the way that God's glory is reflected and displayed. We may start with the core idea of God's kingship, represented by his throne. God, as the great King, rules over the whole universe, assisted by a surrounding court of heavenly beings (angels). Man is made in the image of God. Adam, as a subordinate king under God, rules over the earth, assisted by his fellow human beings. In all these areas, the rule of God is reflected. Now we may transfer these ideas into the analogous area of God's *presence,* his dwelling place, and his appearance. We may start with the heavenly sphere, where God rules, assisted by angelic beings. First, God dwells eternally in himself, through the mystery of the indwelling of the persons of the Trinity (John 14:11). Revelation does not use the language of indwelling, but it presupposes the reality of the Trinity, for we see God and the Lamb sharing the same throne (22:1) and possessing the same name (22:13; 1:8). Second, God dwells in the midst of his heavenly courtiers, surrounded by angels (1 Kings 22:19; Dan. 7:10; Ps. 89:6–7; Rev. 4:4–11; 5:11). Third, God dwells in heaven as his particular abode, but so that he fills all things (1 Kings 8:27, 30; Jer. 23:24). In all these spheres, God displays his glory. The splendor of his magnificence appears in the immediate vicinity of the throne (Rev. 4:3), among the angelic beings (Ezek. 1:16, 22), and in the lights of heaven (Rev. 21:23).

Next, consider the earthly sphere, where man rules over the earth. The high priest, as a model of holiness, displays what is to be reflected in each human being (Ex. 28:17–20). The jewels of the new Jerusalem show what the church as a corporate body is to reflect (Rev. 21:19–20). And the tabernacle and the temple, as special dwelling places of God on earth, display his glory through their beautiful colors and adornments.

We have traced the idea of jewel-like splendor and beauty through its various reflections in the various spheres. The same could be done with almost any of the aspects of God's appearing. For instance, take the throne in verse 2, symbolizing God's authority and power to rule. The angelic beings around God's throne also sit on thrones (v. 4). They have power to rule that derives from and reflects God's power. In the universe as a whole, the heavenly lights rule over the day and the night (Gen. 1:16). On earth, kings have thrones; they have genuine authority deriving from God (Rom. 13:1–5). All believers have the privilege of rule, not only as sons of Adam (Gen. 1:28), but preeminently as sons of God in Christ, who have been given the privilege of sitting with him (Eph. 2:6; Rev. 3:21). Finally, in the earthly tabernacle and temple, the ark of the covenant represents the place from which God rules (Ex. 25:22). The ten commandments deposited in the ark represent the central regulations of God's dominion over Israel (Ex. 25:16).

Similarly, the light of God is reflected in all these spheres. God is himself light (1 John 1:5; Rev. 4:5). The angelic beings appear in a brightness that reflects this uncreated brightness of God (Ezek. 1:13; Rev. 10:1). The heavenly lights reflect God's glory (Rev. 21:23). Human beings rewarded for righteousness wear white robes, individually (Rev. 3:4) and corporately (Rev. 19:8). They are light-bearers, like the lampstands in the tabernacle and the temple (1:12, 20; 11:4).

The rainbow encircling the throne (v. 3) reinforces the theme of light, this time with light of many colors, or perhaps a rainbowlike circle of green (emerald) light. A rainbow similarly appears in Revelation 10:1 and Ezekiel 1:28. The passage in Ezekiel alludes in turn to the original promise of the rainbow in Genesis 9:13–16, which signifies God's mercy and forgiveness of sin.

Now what about the twenty-four elders and their thrones? The heavenly setting suggests that these elders, like the four living creatures (v. 6), are angelic beings, courtiers in God's heavenly court, assistants ready to do his bidding or simply to praise his glory. Old Testament scenes involving God and angelic assistants offer a similar picture (1 Kings 22:19; Dan. 7:10; Ps. 89:6–7; Job

1:6; 2:1). Why, then, are they called "elders," and why are they twenty-four in number?

Some people have suggested that we have here the elders of the church, representing the church in heaven. But in 5:10 the elders speak of the church in the third person, "them," indicating that they are distinct from the church. And in 7:13–14 one of the elders performs an explanatory function, which is typical of angelic beings in this kind of literature (see "Apocalyptic" in the Introduction). They are here called elders because age goes with wisdom (cf. Dan. 7:9). Just as an earthly king has wise men to counsel him on important state decisions, so God has superbly wise counselors as his court attendants.

The number twenty-four is difficult. In 1 Chronicles 24, David organizes the Aaronic priests into twenty-four divisions. Priests are dedicated servants of God's temple on earth. Likewise, God's dwelling in heaven has its dedicated servants, who must be holy and consecrated to qualify them for service. Thus, the twenty-four elders, as heavenly, angelic beings, correspond to the twenty-four divisions of the earthly Aaronic priesthood.

But there is something more to be said. As we have observed, heavenly reality is reflected on earth. Are there then priests now living on earth who may mirror the action of this angelic order of priests? The church on earth is to praise and serve God with the same purity and devotion as this angelic order displays. The church is founded on the twelve apostles (21:14), who correspond to the twelve tribes of Israel (21:12). Hence, with some justification, people have suggested that the twenty-four elders represent the people of God of both the Old and New Testament, symbolizing the twelve tribes and the twelve apostles. The elders are angelic beings, and hence not identical with the church. But they and the church are still images of one another.

The elders have thrones, white robes, and crowns of gold, all of which reflect aspects of God on his throne.

The lightning and thunder (v. 5) exhibit God's power in a manner analogous to the divine appearance on Mount Sinai (Ex. 19:16–19) and elsewhere (Rev. 8:5; 11:19; 16:18; Ps. 18:11–15; Ezek. 1:4). He thus reminds us of the power of his voice (Rev. 1:15; see on 1:10) and the final shaking of creation still to come (11:19; 21:1; Heb. 12:25–27). Lightning and loud noise accompany God's appearing in judgment in Revelation 8:5; 11:19; 16:18. Note the loud noise or voice in 1:10, 15; 5:2, 11–12; 6:1, 10; 7:2, 10; 8:13; 10:3; 11:12, 15; 12:10; 14:2, 7, 9, 15, 18; 16:1, 17; 18:2; 19:1, 6, 17; 21:3.

The **seven lamps** allude to Zechariah 4:2, 6 and Revelation 1:12. The **seven spirits** represent the sevenfold fullness of the Holy Spirit, as in 1:4. The light of the Holy Spirit is the original light of which the seven-branched lampstand of Exodus 25:31–40 was a copy. The similarities with 1:12 suggest that the seven churches, as a true temple of God, are to give out light reflecting the very presence of God through his Spirit.

What is the **sea of glass** (v. 6)? See Revelation 15:2 and Exodus 24:10. This imagery might suggest a number of associations. The parallel verse in 15:2 calls to mind the waters of the Red Sea. The defeat of Pharaoh and the pushing back of the waters foreshadowed God's final victory over evil (Isa. 51:9–11). If so, the sea of glass pictures waters utterly subdued under God's power. Moreover, the extent and beauty of the crystal-like sea, when taken together with the precious stones in 4:3 and 21:18–21, suggest the magnificence and preciousness of God's throne. The numerous parallels elsewhere with the temple might suggest that this sea is the heavenly counterpart of the sea in Solomon's temple (1 Kings 7:23–25). Finally, the picture of heavenly water might simply suggest that God faithfully supplies water from heaven (Deut. 11:11). Which of these various allusions shall we choose? Perhaps all or nearly all should be included. It is consistent with the style of Revelation to weave together a multitude of Old Testament images.

The **four living creatures,** like the twenty-four elders, form
a circle of angelic beings serving in God's throne room. In the
ancient Near East, kings' thrones or palaces often had statues
of winged lions or winged bulls that stood as guardians of the
king's presence. In the Bible, cherubim function both as
guardians of God's holiness (Gen. 3:24; Ex. 25:17–22; 26:31)
and as chariot-bearers of his throne (1 Chron. 28:18; Ps.
18:10). The four living creatures in Revelation are reminiscent
of the living creatures or cherubim in Ezekiel 1 and 10 and the
seraphim in Isaiah 6. The cherubim in the Old Testament are
closely associated with God's chariot, going with the swiftness of
the wind (Ps. 18:10). They are, as it were, the heavenly original
of which earthly winds are an image. They are four in number,
corresponding to the four winds of heaven in the four directions
of the compass (Zech. 6:5; Rev. 7:1). Their eyes, seeing in every
direction (v. 6), mirror the all-seeing eyes of God (Rev. 1:14;
Prov. 15:3; 2 Chron. 16:9).

The four living creatures are, respectively, like a lion, an ox, a
man, and an eagle. Each living creature in Ezekiel 1 has four
faces—of a lion, an ox, a man, and an eagle. The list is the same,
but the creatures in Ezekiel are all identical, with four faces each,
whereas the ones in Revelation are different, each with only one
face. So are these creatures in Revelation distinct from or sub-
stantially identical with the ones in Ezekiel? Revelation constantly utilizes earlier Scripture, but uses it creatively, in new
configurations. Any vision of God and his throne room is less
like a photograph than an artistic impression. It is a *vision,* which
symbolizes rather than photographs the realities that it presents
(cf. Num. 12:6–8). Symbols show us the meaning of things,
rather than merely their physical appearance. But symbols also
warn us that we can never fully fathom who God is. Yes, these
are the heavenly beings of Ezekiel 1, but in a new configuration,
so that we do not exhaustively understand them.

Why do these creatures have the faces of a lion, an ox, a man,
and an eagle? Most likely, they image something of the glory of

God. Among earthly creatures, the lion is the greatest and fiercest of the wild animals, the ox is the strongest of the domesticated animals, the eagle is the most majestic of birds, and man is the ruler over all animals. God is the great and strong ruler over all. His heavenly assistants reflect his attributes. And these heavenly models in turn are reflected in what God has created on earth, not only in the creation of human beings, but in the creation of animals as well. We may often admire and be fascinated by the capacities, skills, and strengths that God has given to animals. How much more awesome are the heavenly beings, and of course God himself! The heavenly beings even now praise God with reverence and eloquence (4:8). Likewise, the destiny of earthly beings, both man and beast, is to join in the praise (5:13–14).

The four living creatures have **six wings,** like the seraphim of Isaiah 6:2, whereas Ezekiel's living creatures have four wings apiece (Ezek. 1:6). The variation again shows the creativity and flexibility in this new vision.

The four living creatures utter a paean of praise for God's holiness (v. 8), like the "Holy, holy, holy" of the seraphim in Isaiah 6:3. God is supremely holy. Here we are at the heart of God's presence. The earthly tabernacle and temple had an outer court, a Holy Place, and a Most Holy Place (literally, "Holy of Holies," Ex. 26:34). These represented different degrees of holiness in the approach to God. Only ceremonially clean Israelites were to enter the outer court. Only priests could enter the Holy Place. Only the high priest could enter the Most Holy Place, but only once a year, with special provisions for cleansing (Lev. 16; Heb. 9:7). But this arrangement, impressive as it was, was only a shadow of God's heavenly presence (Heb. 9:11–12, 23–28). Now we see the real thing, the heavenly original. Fittingly, real cherubim, not merely carved imitations, utter the praise. They celebrate the supreme, unimaginable holiness of God. He is the Almighty, the sovereign ruler. The cherubim creatively build on the seraphic song of Isaiah 6:3 by describing God's lordship over the past, the present, and the future—**who was, and is, and is to come** (as in 1:4). The revelation of God in this vision prepares us for that further coming when he will be manifested in consummation (22:1–5).

The living creatures are answered by the twenty-four elders, as by a kind of antiphonal choir (vv. 10–11). The elders bow down, acknowledging the majesty and authority of God, then pledging their submission, obedience, and reverence. Their crowns, victory wreaths of honor, have meaning only as they are seen as derivative from the One who deserves all honor: "Not to us, O LORD, not to us but to your name be the glory" (Ps. 115:1; cf. 1 Cor. 4:7). Would that not only all our theology but all our motives and conduct were thoroughly animated by this impulse of worship!

As evidence of the supreme worthiness of God, the elders single out his action of creation (v. 11). As Creator, God has absolute mastery, ownership, and control over what he has created. In creation, every speck, every atom, every detail of pattern, the very *being* of everything, derived from the hand of God. His triumph was absolute, his power and wisdom unfathomable, his glory superb. Such, then, are so many displays of God's character in creation. They form a wonderful guarantee that he will continue to be Master, up until the full achievement of his purposes in the consummation (21:5–6; see 1:8). God himself is the ultimate guarantee and refuge for saints in distress or discouragement (Heb. 6:13).

The Triumphant Lamb (5:1–14)

Revelation 4 and 5 are two parts of a single magnificent vision of God's glory (see on 4:1–5:14). A second act within the vision is introduced at 5:1. The focus shifts from creation in 4:11 to redemption and re-creation in 5:1–14. God's purposes of redemption and rule can be accomplished only through one uniquely worthy individual—Jesus Christ. He is simultaneously the fierce Lion of the tribe of Judah, warring against God's enemies (19:11–21; 17:14), and the gentle Lamb that has been slain, who purchased his people with the blood of his atoning sacrifice (5:9–10). Only God in his Trinitarian fullness can achieve these unbelievable purposes. Present are the Father ("him who sat on the throne," 5:1, 7), the Son (the Lamb, 5:6–7), and the Spirit of God (5:6; see 1:4), who is the horns and eyes of the Lamb.

A key element in this vision is the **scroll.** It might represent a number of things—God's covenant, his law, his promises, his plans, or perhaps a legal will. The close parallel with Daniel 12:4 makes it most likely that the scroll is a heavenly book containing God's plan and the destiny of the world. The unsealing of the book implies the accomplishment of the things that God has purposed. John weeps (v. 4) because he longs for God's purposes to be accomplished (cf. Matt. 6:10), but that appears to be impossible. However, through Christ's decisive sacrifice, a whole host is redeemed (v. 9), and the purposes of the Exodus and of man's original dominion are finally fulfilled (v. 10). As a result, all creatures are filled with praise for God and for the Lamb (vv. 11–14).

The section 5:1–14 constitutes the opening scene for the first cycle of judgments that lead up to the second coming of Christ (see "Structure" in the Introduction). The Lamb and the sealed scroll are introduced. The opening of the seals in 6:1–8:1 then sets in motion a series of judgments that have their origin in God's throne and his counsel, and which result in his consummate manifestation (see on 6:12–17 and 8:1).

The scroll in verse 1 contains God's plan for history. It is written on both sides, analogous to the prophetic plans and judgments of Ezekiel 2:9–10. The writing on both sides suggests that the scroll is completely filled. God's plan contains all the details. But it is inaccessible, as the seven seals indicate. No one is worthy to be the channel through which God's plan can become known and be executed—no one except the Lamb. John weeps because he senses the importance of this scroll (v. 4). The destiny of John, of the church, and of the universe itself hangs in the balance over the question of whether someone can open the scroll.

An elder points to some of the qualifications of Christ (v. 5). He is **the Lion of the tribe of Judah,** alluding to the prophecy of Genesis 49:9–10. Jacob, looking toward the future of his twelve sons, prophesies that the ruler will come from Judah. His lionlike characteristics assure all the people of God that he will be strong and fierce and triumphant in fighting enemies. He is also **the Root of David,** alluding to Isaiah 6:13; 11:1. God indicated to David, who belonged to the tribe of Judah, that the line of rule would go through him and his descendants (2 Sam. 7:12–16). The line of descendants beginning with Solomon looks forward to a single great, everlasting king, as Isaiah makes clear. But Jesus is not merely a descendant of David, which would make him merely a branch out of the root. He is himself the root! If we reckon merely by physical descent, the descendant would be expected to be subject to the ancestor. But Jesus is the Son of God as well as the son of David, and that gives him primacy over David in terms of his being, his spiritual qualifications, and his worthiness (cf. Matt. 22:41–46; Ps. 110:1; Isa. 9:6). In fact, in terms of ultimate reckoning, the love of God the Father for his Son is the basis on which God set his love on David and raised him to be king. David exists for the sake of Christ, not the other way around.

After the elder has made his spectacular announcement, one might expect the appearance of a fierce, mighty warrior. Instead, John sees a **Lamb,** and not only a lamb, but one **looking as if it had been slain.** This vision sets forth in dramatic form the central paradox and mystery of the Christian faith. God achieved his triumph and delivered his people, not through the fireworks of military might, but through the weakness of crucifixion. This way of doing things is an offense to worldly ways of thinking:

> For the message of the cross is foolishness to those who are perishing, but to us who are being saved it is the power of God. For

it is written: "I will destroy the wisdom of the wise; the intelligence of the intelligent I will frustrate."

Where is the wise man? Where is the scholar? Where is the philosopher of this age? Has not God made foolish the wisdom of the world? For since in the wisdom of God the world through its wisdom did not know him, God was pleased through the foolishness of what was preached to save those who believe. Jews demand miraculous signs and Greeks look for wisdom, but we preach Christ crucified: a stumbling block to Jews and foolishness to Gentiles, but to those whom God has called, both Jews and Greeks, Christ the power of God and the wisdom of God. (1 Cor. 1:18–24)

Christ's achievement is unique, but it also sets the pattern for Christians. We are to fight our spiritual battles, not with military or political strength, but with endurance, purity, and faithfulness to Christ, even to the point of death. Martyrdom, which looks like defeat to the world, seals the saints' victory, because it appropriates the final victory of Christ in his death and resurrection. "They overcame him by the blood of the Lamb and by the word of their testimony; they did not love their lives so much as to shrink from death" (Rev. 12:11; cf. 11:11–12; 20:4).

The Lamb stands **in the center,** surrounded by the living creatures and the elders, because he is no ordinary servant of God, but the unique mediator of both creation and redemption (Col. 1:13–20), the focal point for all of God's plan (Eph. 1:10). He has **seven horns and seven eyes,** symbolic of his worthiness and ability. Horns frequently represent means of power (Dan. 7:8; 8:3; Pss. 89:17; 92:10), in this case the power of Christ's Spirit-filled, eternal life (1 Cor. 15:45; John 3:34; Rom. 8:11). The **seven spirits of God** are the Holy Spirit in his sevenfold fullness, as in 1:4 and 4:5 (see also Zech. 3:9; 4:10).

The Lamb **took the scroll,** signifying that he is the only one worthy to mediate God's plan. Accordingly, the living creatures and the elders acknowledge his worthiness and praise him. The golden bowls full of incense link up with the incense used in Old

Testament worship (Ex. 30:1–10, 34–38). As burning incense rises up to heaven with a sweet smell, so the prayers of God's people ascend to heaven and are a "sweet smell" to him, acceptable because of the intercession of Christ and the Holy Spirit (Heb. 7:23–25; Rom. 8:26–27).

The song of the living creatures and the elders in verses 9–10 recognizes the worthiness of the Lamb, in harmony with what we have already observed in verses 1–6. The slaying of the Lamb, by crucifixion, is paradoxically the foundation for his triumph and redemption. This triumph through weakness is foolishness to the world, but it was already anticipated in the Exodus, in which the blood of lambs purchased freedom for the sons of Israel. Now there is a new and final purchase, not with animal blood, but with the blood of the Son of God himself:

> He did not enter by means of the blood of goats and calves; but he entered the Most Holy Place once for all by his own blood, having obtained eternal redemption. The blood of goats and bulls and the ashes of a heifer sprinkled on those who are ceremonially unclean sanctify them so that they are outwardly clean. How much more, then, will the blood of Christ, who through the eternal Spirit offered himself unblemished to God, cleanse our consciences from acts that lead to death, so that we may serve the living God! (Heb. 9:12–14; cf. 10:4–10)

Redemption through the Lamb extends not only to the tribes of Israel, but to **every tribe and language and people and nation** (v. 9). In spiritual battle, both God and Satan claim allegiances on a universal scale (7:9; 10:11; 11:9; 12:5; 13:7; 14:6, 8; 15:4; 17:15; 18:3; 19:15; 20:3). But through the merit and power of Christ's sacrifice, God's purposes will be accomplished, fulfilling the Abrahamic promise of blessing for all nations (21:24–27; 7:9–17; Isa. 60:1–5; Gen. 12:3; 22:18). They become **a kingdom and priests,** as in 1:6. Israel was a type, and the fulfillment is an antitype. The unique status that was given to

Israel in Exodus 19:5–6 now extends to all the saints in all nations.

In verses 11–14, praise extends outward. It started with the inner circles represented by the living creatures and the elders. Then the extended hosts of angels take up the praise. And then the earth and its creatures follow suit (v. 13). The destiny of the entire universe is here adumbrated. All things find their fulfillment and the true meaning of their being in a climax of service to God and revelation of his glory.

Opening the Seven Seals (6:1–8:1)

The section 4:1–5:14 represents the heart of the matter, because it shows us God himself. Now the visions start to look at the execution of God's plan. History unfolds as a series of judgments, leading up to the appearing of Christ and the consummation of all things. In 6:1–8:1, we find the first of seven cycles of judgment, each of which leads up to the Second Coming (see "Structure" in the Introduction).

The sealed book determines the judgments in 6:1–8:1. This book appeared in 5:1, and the Lamb took it in 5:7. Now judgments from God's throne unfold as the Lamb opens the seven seals one by one. The participation of the Lamb reminds us that these judgments are based on his unique qualifications and accomplishments (5:1–14). In formal structure, 5:1–8:1 runs parallel to 8:2–11:19. Each has an opening scene introducing the origin of the judgments (5:1–14; 8:2–6). Six judgments follow (6:1–17; 8:7–9:21). A dramatic interlude promises care for God's people (7:1–17; 10:1–11:14). The seventh and climactic judgment follows the interlude (8:1; 11:15–19). (See "Structure" in the Introduction.) The seven judgments move forward toward the Second Coming, which occurs in 6:12–17 and 11:15–19. The first four judgments in each case have an inner unity. The first four seals (6:1–8) involve horsemen, which correspond to the four living creatures of 4:6 and the four horsemen of Zechariah 1:8. The first four trumpets (8:7–12) pertain to the four major regions of the world, namely, dry land, sea, fresh water, and air/sky.

The four horsemen of 6:1–8 represent conquest, war, famine, and death. These calamities characterize an indefinite period before the Second Coming (Mark 13:6–8). Such things occurred during the tumults of the Roman Empire, are occurring now, and may be expected to occur just before the Second Coming. The imagery is capable of multiple embodiments (see "Schools of Interpretation" in the Introduction). The seven churches were exhorted to put their confidence, not in the peace and prosperity supposedly achieved by Roman rule, but in God and his promises of a new world (21:4; 2:17; 3:12). When tumults occurred, they were assured that the Lamb was still in control—in fact, the tumults issued from his breaking of the seals and from the voice of the living creatures. Such judgments represented the chastening hand of God on a rebellious world (cf. 9:20–21). The saints would be cared for in the midst of such trials (7:1–17). They were sealed as a mark of ownership and protection (7:1–10; 9:4) and were given perfect rest in the end (7:15–17).

Such promises hold for the saints throughout the church age, not just for the seven churches. We today are to put our hope in the Lamb, not in earthly promises of prosperity and security. When calamities come, we may remain calm, knowing that the Lamb who was slain for us is still in control (Rom. 8:28–39).

The First Seal: The White Horse of Conquest (6:1–2)

The Lamb, who alone is worthy to do so, opens the seals one by one. In everyday life, the contents of a sealed scroll would be accessible only after all the seals were open. However, here we have a vision. For dramatic effect, the plan of God, as contained in the scroll, begins to unfold with the opening of the first seal. The living creatures, as servants of God and the Lamb, participate in the action. Angelic assistants may be involved in many aspects of world history, without our being aware of their role. The perspective from earth is always incomplete, as in Job's case.

A white horse goes forth, representing conquest, the first of four calamities issuing from the four seals. On the basis of similarities with 19:11, some think that Christ appears here, conquering through the gospel. But the white horse must be similar in character to the other three horses. Together they form a foursome, analogous to Zechariah 1:8; 6:1–3. In many places in Revelation, white symbolizes purity, but in the first century it could also symbolize victory, which is the point here. Conquest can sometimes be bloodless, but it can also take the form of bloody war, as in the next calamity (vv. 3–4).

According to our interpretation of Revelation (see "Schools of Interpretation" in the Introduction), the prophecies here have multiple embodiments. In the first century, the Roman Empire maintained control through conquest, which could include bloodshed and ensuing famine and death. Roman peace promised prosperity, but the reality was different. Conquest, bloodshed, famine, and death have also stalked the human race throughout the church age, and they may be expected to intensify in the final crisis leading to the Second Coming.

The Second Seal: The Red Horse of Slaughter (6:3–4)

From the Lamb and the second living creature comes now a second calamity, namely slaughter. War is the most obvious form of slaughter (Mark 13:7), but the picture is broad enough to encompass other forms of human slaughter. The fiery red color echoes the fire of God's judgment seen in 4:5 and 1:14, but also represents the red blood that will come from the slaughter.

The Third Seal: The Black Horse of Famine (6:5–6)

The third horse brings famine. For the average laborer, **a day's wages** (a denarius) bought only enough wheat to eat for the day. In the ancient world, barley was cheaper, but also of lower quality. It was eaten by the poor. A laborer with a family to support was forced to a subsistence level. In the vision, oil and wine are spared, indicating the partial nature of the famine. But wheat and barley were the primary foods needed to survive.

The Fourth Seal: The Pale Horse of Death (6:7–8)

The fourth horse is pale, symbolizing terror. Its rider is named **Death,** and **Hades** (the abode of the dead) follows him. The fourth calamity is the most terrible yet, and includes many features of the preceding three. The four categories mentioned—death, famine, pestilence, and wild beasts—echo Ezekiel 14:21. The calamities grow in intensity, leading up to the final judgment of the Second Coming. But as yet there is still a limit: only **a fourth of the earth** is affected.

The Fifth Seal: The Cry of the Martyrs (6:9–11)

When hearing these frightening descriptions, saints may well wonder what is to become of them in the midst of calamities. God gives a partial answer through a vision of martyrs (see 1:2; 2:10, 13). Martyred saints cry out for justice, not because of selfish desires, but in tune with the justice of God's throne (v. 10). They desire to see God's justice fully manifested and evil eliminated. **The inhabitants of the earth** form a group opposing God. Humanity consists of two groups: the people of God, whose citizenship is in heaven (Phil. 3:20), and, in opposition to them, the rebellious inhabitants of the earth (6:15; 8:13; 11:10; 13:3, 8, 12, 14; 17:2, 8). Although the picture focuses specifically on martyrs, it applies to all faithful believers. Jesus calls on all his followers to surrender their life in order that they may gain eternal life (Matt. 16:24–26; Luke 9:23–26; John 12:25).

Final judgment does not come immediately, but only in God's time (Rev. 6:11; 22:7, 10–12, 17; Luke 18:1–8).

The Sixth Seal: The Second Coming (6:12–17)

With the opening of the sixth seal, all dwellers on earth and the cosmos itself experience God's judgment. Verses 12–17 give the first of seven descriptions in Revelation of events associated with the Second Coming (see "Structure" in the Introduction). In Luke 21:25–27 and Mark 13:24–26, the coming of the Son of Man immediately follows phenomena in the sun, the moon, and the stars. The mention of seven types of people (6:15) suggests complete judgment, as does the announcement of "the great day of their wrath" (6:17). Since this world is to be so thoroughly shaken, the saints must hope in God (Heb. 12:25–29; Luke 12:32–34; 1 Cor. 7:29–31).

An earthquake indicates that God is coming, and that the very foundations of the creation respond to his presence (cf. Rev. 8:5; 11:19; 16:18; Mark 13:8; Ex. 19:18; Isa. 29:6; Matt. 27:54). Phenomena in the heavens indicate the shaking of the old order of the first creation, in preparation for the coming of the new creation (Rev. 21:1; 2 Peter 3:10–14; Matt. 24:29–30; Isa. 13:10; 24:23). People of all types recognize that the judgment of God is coming. They finally come to the point of fearing judgment, but with terror rather than with repentance. Like Adam and Eve (Gen. 3:8), they can only think of fleeing and hiding to avoid exposure and punishment (cf. Luke 23:30; Hos. 10:8; Isa. 2:19).

The saints, on the other hand, may look forward to the day of Christ with anticipation. It represents their vindication and the suppression of wickedness. It is **the great day of [God's] wrath,** a time when the just anger of God is revealed against the evils and corruptions that have spread on earth (cf. Gen. 6).

Interlude: Protection for the Saints (7:1–17)

The announcement of the seventh seal is dramatically delayed while the saints receive assurance that God knows them and protects them (v. 3) in the midst of the calamities depicted in chapter 6. They are sealed from harm as in Ezekiel 9:4. The focus is on protection from *spiritual* harm, since it is clear in Revelation that they may suffer persecution and sometimes death for the sake of their faith (Rev. 2:10, 13; 13:15). The interlude contains two complementary pictures: the vision of the 144,000 in 7:1–8 and the vision of the great multitude in 7:9–17. These visions picture God's protection of his people, but from two different perspectives. The numbering in 7:1–8 links God's people with their Israelite heritage, and emphasizes that God knows and cares for each one of them. The same group, though numbered by God, is so vast as to be beyond human numbering (v. 9). They come from every nation, not only through biological descent from Jacob. They are victorious, secure, and comforted on the other side of **the great tribulation** (v. 14).

The 144,000 (7:1–8)

Four angels hold back the four winds, symbolizing that God is holding back calamities until after his people are sealed. The sealing guarantees their protection when the calamities are unleashed (cf. 9:4; Ezek. 9:4). The seal confirms both God's ownership and his protection (cf. 9:4; 14:1; 3:12).

The number of the sealed comes to 12,000 for each tribe. The balanced numbers suggests that twelve is a symbolic number for the fullness of the people of God. Dan is omitted, possibly because it was early associated with idolatry (Judg. 18; cf. Rev. 22:15; 21:8). Instead, we find both the tribe of Joseph and the tribe of Manasseh. Now Manasseh and Ephraim were the two sons of Joseph. Hence, logically, we should find either Joseph listed alone, or Manasseh and Ephraim listed separately. The oddity of mentioning both Joseph and Manasseh again suggests that the list is symbolic. Some think that the 144,000 consist only of Jewish believers. But the expression "the servants of our God" in 7:3 must include Gentile saints as well. The equal status of Jews and Gentiles in the seven churches (see Eph. 2:11–22) and the promises associated only with the 144,000 (Rev. 9:4; 14:1–5) confirm it. According to 7:1–8, the saints are known by God one by one, and none slips by his care (cf. Matt. 10:30).

The Great Multitude (7:9–17)

If 7:1–8 emphasizes the Israelite heritage of the New Testament people of God, then 7:9–17 emphasizes their international character. They are **a great multitude . . . from every nation, tribe, people and language,** fulfilling the promise to Abraham that all the peoples on earth would be blessed through him (Gen. 12:3; 17:5).

Holding palm branches as a sign of joyous celebration (cf. John 12:13), they praise God, whose salvation they have received. As in the scene pictured in 4:1–5:14, many beings join in the praise.

The victors, the whole people of God, **have come out of the great tribulation** (v. 14). Many identify the great tribulation with a final period of persecution shortly before the Second Coming. But tribulations for Christians occur throughout the church age, so that the whole age can be characterized as one of tribulation (2 Thess. 1:5–6; 2 Tim. 3:1, 12). Thus, this passage provides comfort to first-century Christians as well as to those in the final crisis (see 11:2).

The white robes of purity and honor belong to the multitude, not because of anything that they have achieved through their own power, but through the power of Christ's redemption. In a startling juxtaposition, his blood washes them white (cf. Zech. 13:1; Isa. 4:4; Heb. 9:14; 1 John 1:7).

The victorious saints appear before God to enjoy his presence in blissful peace and comfort (vv. 15–17). At the heart of blessing is the presence of God and the Lamb, and their care for the saints. The picture here anticipates the final peace of 21:1–4; 22:1–5. Since 6:12–17 has already taken us up to the Second Coming, the next event would be the appearing of the new Jerusalem and its blessings. But Revelation is not ready at this early point in its dramatic development to expose fully God's plans for the new world. At this point, it suffices that the saints receive his promise in general terms.

The Seventh Seal: Silence in Heaven (8:1)

What happens with the opening of the seventh seal? We expect the seventh one to be climactic. Seven symbolizes completeness; so, with the seventh seal, we should complete our travel through history. The phenomena accompanying the Second Coming occur after the opening of the sixth seal (6:12–17). So now we wait for a description of the actual appearing of Christ (cf. Mark 13:24–26), the final judgment, and the new heaven and the new earth. What actually takes place seems anticlimactic: there is simply silence. Some interpreters have seen this silence as a blank, which is then filled with the contents of the trumpets (8:2–11:19). But it is difficult to find such a use of silence in ancient literature, and it does not fit the tempo of Revelation, in which 6:12–17 already brings the Second Coming. Therefore, it is better to understand the trumpets as beginning another cycle of events, looking back over times earlier than 6:12–17.

Within a framework of biblical symbolism, the silence most naturally indicates that heaven stands in awe at the presence of God (cf. Hab. 2:20; Zeph. 1:7). God appears. His awesome appearance is the central reality. At this early point, the seer is not given a fuller picture either of God or of the events accompanying the final judgment and re-creation. This reserve maintains the reader's interest for later cycles of judgment.

The Seven Trumpets (8:2–11:19)

Seven angels blow seven trumpets. The trumpets set in motion seven judgments leading up to the Second Coming (see "Structure" in the Introduction). The trumpets form the second cycle out of several that depict God's rule over history from various angles. Like the trumpets used in the battle of Jericho (Josh. 6), these trumpets lead to the fall of the worldly city (Rev. 11:13). And in the seventh trumpet, the complete victory of God arrives. The trumpet plagues are reminiscent of the plagues on Egypt, signifying God's judgments on idolatrous power.

The seven seals began with announcements of riders commissioned to bring calamities (6:1–8). The seven trumpets, by contrast, contain vivid descriptions of the calamities themselves. The intensity of judgment has increased. Yet some things are still spared: most of the plagues fall on only a third of the region; the locust plague of 9:1–12 is over after five months; some people survive the collapse of the city in 11:13. By contrast, the later judgments with the bowls (15:1–16:21) are thoroughly devastating.

The first four trumpet plagues (8:7–12) strike the four major regions of creation: dry land, sea, fresh water, and sky. The first four bowls affect the same four regions (16:1–9). The trumpet plagues strike one-third of the region, indicating a less intense judgment than the corresponding bowl judgments. In this way, the judgments in Revelation build up in intensity and increasingly focus on the Second Coming, until 19:11–20:15 is reached (fig. 17).

FIG. 17. INTENSIFICATION OF JUDGMENTS,
FROM TRUMPETS TO BOWLS

Trumpets	Bowls
One-third of the land	*All* land
One-third of the sea	*All* sea
Bitter drinking	Drinking blood
One-third of the heavenly bodies	The sun

Within the period of the early church, these visions were fulfilled both through natural calamities and through analogous spiritual calamities afflicting the souls of the wicked. In apocalyptic imagery, the one type of calamity can represent the other. The general principles can be applied more broadly (see "Schools of Interpretation" in the Introduction). Both human beings and the natural world undergo stress until the time of final renewal (Rom. 8:18–25). The natural world, as well as humanity, is affected by the Second Coming (2 Peter 3:10, 12).

The Angels with the Seven Trumpets (8:2–6)

The trumpet judgments issue from God's angels, who stand before his throne (v. 2). The vision of 4:1–5:14 remains an anchor point for this new cycle of visions. Like the seal judgments of 6:1–8:1, these judgments are executed according to God's plan and in accordance with his orders. The prayers of the saints play a notable part in initiating the judgments (8:3–4; cf. 5:8). Regarding thunder and other rumbling, lightning, and an earthquake (v. 5), see 4:5 and 6:12.

The First Four Trumpets (8:7–13)

Now consider the first four trumpets. For the first trumpet **hail and fire** (v. 7) are reminiscent of the seventh Egyptian plague in Exodus 9:23–24. As in the case of the Egyptian plagues, these judgments come from God against evildoers. They show that God is the true God, and they call people to repentance. Yet, like the Egyptians, people may harden themselves and not repent (cf. Rev. 9:20–21). Some other trumpet plagues parallel other Egyptian plagues (fig. 18).

Fig. 18. Trumpet Plagues and Their Parallels in Exodus

Trumpet	Plague	Parallel in Exodus
1st—8:7	hail and fire	7th—hail and fire
2nd—8:8–9	blood	1st—blood
3rd—8:10–11	bitter water	
4th—8:12	darkness	9th—darkness
5th—9:1–11	locusts	8th—locusts
6th—9:13–21	army	
7th—11:15–19	storm	Ex. 19:16–19

After the fourth trumpet, an eagle appears, indicating that even more terrible judgments follow in the last three plagues (v. 13). He announces **woe,** a typical beginning to a prophetic oracle (for example, see Amos 5:18; 6:1). The three last trumpets are grouped together as three woes (9:12; 11:14). These plagues explicitly discriminate between the righteous and the wicked, as did the later Egyptian plagues.

The Fifth Trumpet: Locusts (9:1–12)

The fifth trumpet blast sets in motion a horrific army of locusts, energized by demonic powers (9:1–2). This imagery derives from Exodus 10:13–15 and from Joel 2:1–11, where a literal locust plague foreshadows even more devastating judgment coming from a divinely commissioned army (Joel 2:11). Their terrorizing powers compare only to those of the Beast (Rev. 13:1–10). These infernal monsters attack only the wicked, not the saints (9:4).

The wicked sometimes suffer in this life in a way that presages their final punishment (20:11–15). This vision depicts the self-defeating and tormenting nature of wickedness in the human soul. This general principle has multiple fulfillments (see

"Schools of Interpretation" in the Introduction). Within the Roman Empire, it represents how people who worship idols and worship the emperor suffer torments of soul. In addition, as God brings the structures of the Empire under judgment, people may experience suffering through social, political, and military failures as well. In the future, just before the Second Coming, judgments of God against the wicked will intensify. Also, the general principle applies to the entire church age. Wickedness brings suffering rather than the desired success (cf. Prov. 10:6–7, 9, 11, etc.). Like Proverbs, Revelation delineates a general pattern. But it also recognizes that the saints may for a time suffer grievously (6:9–10). Within this world order, justice does not always triumph quickly.

The locusts operate for **five months** (v. 5). A normal locust swarm would move on after a few days. This demonic swarm stays for the whole period during which locusts might be seen, emphasizing the severity of this judgment. Their leader is **Apollyon** (Hebrew, **Abaddon**), which means "destroyer." There may be an ironic allusion here to Nero or Domitian, both of whom saw themselves as imitators of the Greek god Apollo.

The Sixth Trumpet: The Conquering Army (9:13–21)

The Roman Empire feared an attack of the Parthians from beyond the Euphrates (9:14), the eastern border of the Empire. But all such fears are dwarfed by what Revelation pictures. Such outside threats presage the final day of battle, which will be of cosmic proportions (16:14). The warfare of 9:13–21 is similar to that of 16:14, but the consequences are less severe, still leaving time for repentance (9:18–21). Nations as well as individuals who give themselves to idols or to the worship of power and conquest may find themselves overwhelmed in a military judgment brought against them. It happened to ancient Babylon, to Greece, to Rome, to Hitler's Third Reich, and to the Soviet Union.

Interlude: The Witness of the Saints (10:1–11:14)

Between the sixth and seventh trumpets stands an interlude (10:1–11:14) with two scenes. Both scenes are concerned with the role of God's people and their prophetic witness during a time of trial. In the first scene (10:1–11), John receives prophetic messages and is commissioned to proclaim them. The second (11:1–14) depicts the history of the two witnesses and their larger environment.

The Little Scroll Given to John (10:1–11)

The section 10:1–11 has parallels to Daniel 10:5–6 and to the call of Ezekiel in Ezekiel 2:1–3:11. John receives the prophetic messages of **a little scroll.** Some have thought that the scroll contains the contents of Revelation 12:1–22:5, and that 12:1 begins a new major division in the structure of the book. More likely, the vision of 10:1–11 speaks in a general fashion of John's being empowered to continue to prophesy. Although John's role is unique, he is still in many ways an example and a pattern for the church's witness (see 1:2). We must take to heart the message of John (1:3), live by it, and be ready to communicate its implications to "peoples, nations, languages and kings" (10:11).

First a mighty angel appears, reflecting the very glory of God and his throne room (vv. 1–2; cf. 1:12–16; Dan. 10:5–6; Ezek. 1:27–28). His majesty underlines the authority and divine source of his message.

Seven thunders speak, but John cannot tell us what their content is (vv. 3–4). In Revelation, God reveals the substance of his plan, but keeps many aspects and details of it hidden (Deut. 29:29). We must be content to trust God in the midst of our partial knowledge, confident that he knows everything and governs everything for our benefit (Rom. 8:28–39).

The announcement of **no more delay** (v. 6) indicates that the consummation of God's plans comes with the seventh trumpet. Like the cycle of seven seals, the cycle of seven trumpets leads up to the Second Coming. Here the angel's announcement emphasizes the significance of the Second Coming as the wrapping up of God's plan for history (cf. Eph. 1:10).

John takes and eats the little scroll, in a manner parallel to Ezekiel 2:3–3:9, indicating that God commissions him with the Ezekiel-like task of prophesying woe to an unrepentant world. The scroll will **turn your stomach sour.** That is, the contents of the scroll contain much news of suffering. At the same time, it is **as sweet as honey** in the mouth (cf. Ezek. 3:3; Pss. 119:103; 19:10). The word of God provides communion with him and his goodness; hence, sweetness accompanies even a message of woe.

The Two Witnesses (11:1–14)

The second part of the interlude in 10:1–11:14 tells the story of two witnesses. Like Moses and Elijah, these witnesses perform striking miracles (vv. 5–6). They are said to be the two olive trees and the two lampstands (v. 4), which recalls the vision of Zechariah 4:1–14, in which the trees probably symbolize the ruling and priestly offices of Zerubbabel and Joshua. Thus, the witnesses are prominent representatives of God. Their stand against the Beast (vv. 7–10) reminds us of the struggles against bestial kingdoms in Daniel. Verse 8 reminds us of wicked, oppressive cities and powers: Sodom, Egypt, and the Jerusalem that crucified Jesus. The resurrection in verses 11–12 reminds us of Christ's resurrection, but also of Ezekiel 37 and the rapture of Elijah.

Like John in 10:1–11, the two witnesses are models for all the saints to imitate. All of us are to be faithful to the testimony of Jesus, even in the face of violent persecution from the Beast. We must be willing to face martyrdom, and God guarantees our vindication (vv. 11–12).

Some aspects of this vision remain difficult and controversial. Some interpreters think that two specific human beings are in view: either two Christian prophets who were martyred shortly before the fall of Jerusalem, or two prophets who will appear shortly before the Second Coming. However, in agreement with Revelation as a whole, we find here a symbolic representation of Christian witness. The two witnesses are said to be two lamp-stands (v. 4), which indicates that they are symbolic figures. They represent the witnessing church, just as the seven lampstands in 1:12, 20 represent the seven churches of 1:11. Here two lamp-stands are mentioned rather than seven in order to imitate the pattern of Zechariah 4 and to reflect the pairing of Moses and Elijah (Matt. 17:3–4; cf. Deut. 17:6; Luke 10:1).

The trampling of the city for forty-two months has sometimes been correlated with the fall of Jerusalem in A.D. 70. But a closer look shows that the events do not correspond in detail. Verse 1 indicates that the inner part, the temple and the altar, are pre-served. And nothing that we know about the fall of Jerusalem corresponds exactly to the two witnesses. Instead, 11:1–14 gives a general visionary representation of the witness of the church and of God's preservation and vindication of that witness.

The temple represents the presence of God on earth, espe-cially through his people (see the note on 4:1–5:14). Measurement signifies God's knowledge and care (cf. Ezek. 40–41). The altar and those who worship there represent the true worshipers of God, who are sealed and protected (cf. 7:1–17). The destruction of the outer court represents the at-tack of outsiders on God's people.

What do the **42 months** mean? This is a limited time of dis-tress and intense conflict between God's people and their op-ponents (13:5). It is also described as 1,260 days (11:3; 12:6), or as a time, times, and half a time (12:14), which means three and a half years. (In a symbolic context like this one, a month is reckoned as consisting of 30 days.) This is half of seven years, which suggests a complete period of suffering, cut short by half. The main background for this is found in Daniel 7:25, which in turn is related to other passages in Daniel (9:27; 12:7, 11–12). Some futurist interpreters look for a period of time of this length shortly before the Second Coming. But, like other numbers in

Revelation, this one is symbolic. It is related to the three and a half days mentioned in 11:9, 11. Thus, it designates a period of persecution of limited length.

The most significant clue comes from Daniel 9:27. In Daniel 9, God sets out a period of seventy weeks or 490 years or ten jubilee cycles, during which he will accomplish his purposes for worldwide redemption (Dan. 9:24). This period of seventy weeks builds on the earlier period of seventy years of exile prophesied by Jeremiah (Dan. 9:2; Jer. 25:12; 29:10). Each of Jeremiah's seventy years is a sabbatical year in which the land rests (2 Chron. 36:21; Lev. 26:43; 25:1–7). Hence, it represents a total of 490 years. At the end of this period, God favors Israel again and restores his people to the land and to Jerusalem (Ezra 1:1–4; 2 Chron. 36:22–23). But this restoration is only preliminary. The final restoration takes place at the conclusion of a second period of 490 years. And since the whole sabbath pattern symbolizes final rest, it is fitting that this second period consists of *symbolic years,* symbolizing the way to the consummation. The consummation occurs at the end of 490 symbolic years. The last week of years, seven symbolic years, stands for the time of inaugurated eschatology, after the Messiah has come and accomplished redemption (Dan. 9:26a). In the middle of the last week, the sanctuary is destroyed (Dan. 9:27), which took place in A.D. 70. The period from 70 to the Second Coming is the last half week of Daniel's prophecy, a period of trouble and persecution as in Daniel 7:25. The 1,260 days, then, cover the entire interadvental period, viewed as a time of persecution and distress (cf. 2 Tim. 3:1–13; 2 Thess. 1:4–8).[19]

Like John's other visions, this one has multiple applications throughout the church age. For the seven churches in their first century context, it indicates that persecution will come, but will be limited in length and will end in vindication (vv. 11–12). It likewise holds out the same promise for Christians throughout the ages. Just before the Second Coming, we are to expect a violent crisis that will bring intense conflict and persecution (2 Thess. 2:1–12).

The two witnesses perform miraculous signs of judgment, in a manner reminiscent of Moses and Elijah, two great miracle-working prophets in the Old Testament (vv. 5–6). Like Moses and Elijah, the church bears prophetic witness. We call people to repentance and warn of coming judgment. Our total message includes not only good news of salvation in Christ, but also the revelation of God's character, which implies that judgment against evildoers is inevitable. Our message is one of power—power to save and power to punish (2 Cor. 2:15–17; Rom. 1:16). It is not an arbitrary power, to do with as we see fit, but a power that comes from God, which we exercise only as servants who proclaim a message that we cannot alter (Eph. 2:6–7; 2 Cor. 3:5–6; 6:6–7; 10:4–6).

The Beast in 11:7 represents demonized state power persecuting the church (see 13:1–10 and "Counterfeiting" in the Introduction). Satan energizes false worship and stirs up opposition to the true message, trying to destroy Christians and snuff out their witness (12:13–13:10). Persecution and martyrdom throughout history are all of a piece, as verse 8 reminds us. Whether in Sodom (Gen. 19), in Egypt (Ex. 1–15), or in Jerusalem (at Christ's death), the enemies of God oppose him and his people. The witness of God's people is odious to God's enemies, because they prefer the darkness (John 3:17–21). Instead of receiving the church's witness gratefully, they experience it as a torment (v. 10).

The picture given here is extreme, and for good reason. In most of life, when people examine their conscious motives, they find confusing mixtures. The saints are followers of Christ, but their obedience is flawed and inconsistent. Non-Christians are in rebellion against God, but their rebellion is likewise inconsistent. They are not as bad as they could be, but are restrained in mysterious ways. They find themselves, albeit from wrong motives, admiring and imitating some of the good that they see around them. But this mixture of motives can easily obscure the seriousness of the most fundamental conflict in history, that between God and his enemies. Revelation puts the spotlight on this fundamental conflict, and therefore depicts good and evil in black-and-white fashion. The two witnesses are supremely powerful witnesses. Conversely, their opponents are supremely hostile opponents. The inhabitants of earth not only want to see the witnesses dead, but unashamedly rejoice and celebrate their death, indicating the full hardness of their position (vv. 9–10). Such polarization of allegiance is the reality of our world at a fundamental level. Revelation gives us a look behind the obscuring curtain of civilizing and moderating ploys that conceal our deepest allegiances.

This lesson is very important. In your own life, look for the deadly conflict and persevere unflinchingly in witness and loyalty to Christ. In the lives of non-Christians, look beneath the veneer of pleasantries and see the deadly opposition that only divine power can stop. Witness is a powerful factor in spiritual war. But it fails to win unless God renews people's hearts.

The scene is **the great city,** the worldly city, which includes not only Sodom and Egypt of old, and not only Jerusalem, but also Rome, each of the seven cities in Asia Minor, and our modern cities today. It is the city bent on independence from God's way, as was Babel of old (Gen. 11:1–9). The war between the two cities, the city of God (Heb. 12:22–29; 11:16) and the city of man, continues throughout history until Babel/Babylon is finally destroyed (Rev. 17–18) and the new Jerusalem comes to consummation (21:1–22:5).

The bodies of the two witnesses lie unburied for **three and a half days** (vv. 9, 11). This repeats on a smaller scale the period of three and a half years (12:14; see on 11:2), or forty-two months, in which the saints experience persecution. By analogy, the three and a half days are a period of such intense persecution that the witness of the church seems to be completely snuffed out. The two witnesses are killed by the Beast. Not only in the Roman Empire, but nowadays, and in the final crisis, faithful witnesses sometimes seem to go down in defeat. Christians are all in prison or dead, and apparently the idolatrous state has triumphed. The anti-Christian tyrant is in control, whether Domitian or Diocletian or the Spanish Inquisition or North Korean communism or Saudi Arabia's Islamic state. But note: three and a half days are seven days cut in half, signifying that domination that aspires to completeness is cut off halfway through. Moreover, this period of three and a half days reminds us of the three days of Christ's suffering (Matt. 12:40; Mark 8:31). Christ's martyrdom and resurrection provide the pattern, the firstfruits (1 Cor. 15:23, 49). We who belong to Christ cannot but share in his victory. So the martyr's death is not defeat, but victory in union with Christ.

The Seventh Trumpet: God's Temple Opened (11:15–19)

The second cycle of judgments (8:2–11:19) closes with a second description of the Second Coming. It zeroes in on the Last Judgment (11:18) and the triumph of God's rule (vv. 15, 17). The opening of God's temple in heaven is the opening of the original of which the earthly temple was a copy. The **ark** is seen (v. 19). The ark was the most holy object in the tabernacle (Ex. 25:10–22). It was normally concealed from sight behind the tabernacle curtains. The revealing of this innermost object signifies that God has fully revealed his glory, both the glory of his law (the covenant words) and of his mercy (as signified by the atonement cover).

All in all, this opening implies the revealing of God himself. Lightning, thunder, and other awesome natural phenomena accompany his appearing (v. 19), as at Mount Sinai, showing the majesty of his power. With God's presence comes also the renewal of all things (21:1–22:5). But the further explanation of this renewal must wait for a later point in the dramatic development in Revelation (see "Structure" in the Introduction).

Seven Symbolic Histories (12:1–14:20)

We have examined the first two cycles of judgments, the seven seals (6:1–8:1) and the seven trumpets (8:2–11:19). Now we begin the third cycle. This third cycle of visions consists primarily of histories of key symbolic characters: the Dragon, the Woman, the Beast, the False Prophet, the 144,000, angelic announcers, and the Son of Man (see "Structure" in the Introduction). Unlike the seven seals and the seven trumpets, these visions have no explicit numbering. But like the preceding cycles, they lead up to a vision of the Second Coming (14:14–20). The two preceding cycles focused on the judgments issuing from God's throne. This cycle depicts in depth the nature of the spiritual conflict. Characters appear in symbolic form to represent the forces on the two sides of a cosmic spiritual war.

God himself has already been revealed in 4:1–5:14. Opposing him are Satan (the Dragon) and his agents, the Beast (13:1–10) and the False Prophet (13:11–18; see 16:13). On God's side are his people, portrayed as a light-bearing woman (12:1–6, 13–17) and as a chaste, numbered, and protected multitude (14:1–5). These two complementary pictures show the saints in their capacity as witnesses of God's light and as separated from the corruptions of the world. Thus, the saints are exhorted to remain faithful to Christ in opposition to the persecution of the Beast, and to remain pure in opposition to the seduction of the Prostitute (see "Counterfeiting" in the Introduction). These symbolic pictures show the two sides stripped of all inconsistency and confusion, so that we may better understand the nature of our warfare (cf. Eph. 6:10–20). The present conflicts will be superseded by the peace of 21:1–22:5 when the consummation of God's plans takes effect.

Like the first two cycles, this one consists of four parts (see "Structure" in the Introduction). An opening scene introduces the characters (12:1–6). Then follow six symbolic histories (12:7–14:11). After an interlude (14:12–13) comes the seventh, climactic history (14:14–20). There are thus seven symbolic histories in all: the history of the Dragon (12:7–12), the history of the woman (12:13–17), the history of the Beast (13:1–10), the history of the False Prophet (13:11–18), the history of the 144,000 (14:1–5), the history of the angelic proclaimers (14:6–11), and the history of the coming of the Son of Man (14:14–20).

The Woman and the Dragon (12:1–6)

As the scene opens, a woman appears, arrayed in cosmic light. The imagery calls to mind Joseph's dream (Gen. 37:9–10) and the picture of Jerusalem giving birth to the Messiah and his remnant (Mic. 5:3; Isa. 54:1–4; 66:7–13). The Old Testament saints collectively are in view. Mary, the mother of Jesus, is included in this group, but only as an outstanding member of it. Later, it appears that the New Testament saints are also included (12:13–17). The light-bearing character of the woman foreshadows the glory of the new Jerusalem (21:11, 22–27). She has her citizenship in heaven (Phil. 3:20) and receives the splendor and importance of heaven. In her privileges, the church already partakes of the blessings that are to come. But she is still buffeted by Satan.

Opposing the woman is **an enormous red dragon.** Our chief opponent is not some earthly power. We struggle "against the rulers, against the authorities, against the powers of this dark world and against the spiritual forces of evil in the heavenly realms" (Eph. 6:12), at the head of which is Satan (Eph. 2:2; 2 Cor. 4:4). The Dragon is identified as Satan, the Devil, in 12:9. The image of a dragon shows that Satan has enormous power and hideous enmity against God. Satan has constantly opposed the plans of God and has been repeatedly defeated in the great acts of his saving power (Gen. 3:1, 15; Ps. 74:13–14; Isa. 27:1; 51:9–10; Ezek. 29:3; Luke 10:18; 11:14–23; John 12:31; Col. 2:15). Now he rises against the Messiah (Rev. 12:4–5) and his servants (12:17), but will suffer final destruction (20:10). The ancient Near East had certain myths about a sea monster or water god producing chaos. Polytheistic myths dimly sensed the threat of satanic chaos, but in their confused groping they never penetrated to the reality.

The Dragon has seven heads, increasing his hideousness. In Daniel and Revelation, multiple heads often symbolize multiple manifestations of a single kingdom. In the same way, Satan manifests his power through multiple channels and in multiple institutions and events. Seven, the number of completeness, suggests that the Dragon has extensive power and many manifestations. He aspires blasphemously to imitate the completeness of God.

The Dragon's tail **swept a third of the stars out of the sky.** The Dragon attacks God's order and rule, symbolized by the order of the stars. He assaults heaven itself, symbolized by the effect on the heavenly bodies. This verse has given rise to speculation that a third of the angels fell and became demons at the time that Satan rebelled against God. But the Bible provides few clues about the fall of Satan and his angels. The immediate focus of verse 4 is not on Satan's original act of rebellion, but on his attack on the **male child** (v. 5). In the background lies Daniel 8:10, which predicts the attack of Antiochus Epiphanes on the Jewish people and their temple. Against this background, the stars may symbolize the angelic representatives of the church in its heavenly character (note the stars in Rev. 12:1, and Michael and his angels in 12:7).[20]

The woman **gave birth to a son,** in fulfillment of Micah 5:3. Christ is born, and his triumphant rule over the nations is certain to be established.

Satan attempts to destroy the child as soon as he is born, as Herod did in Matthew 2:1–18. Herod's action was the first in a series of satanically engineered attempts to prevent the accomplishment of God's salvation. Satan tempted Christ in the wilderness (Matt. 4:1–11; Luke 4:1–13) and was active in the background when Christ cast out demons and confronted opposition from Jewish leaders. Revelation encapsulates all this opposition in the single picture of Satan seeking to devour the child. Passing over Jesus' earthly life, it arrives immediately at the ascension and enthronement of the Messiah: **her child was snatched up to God and to his throne.** The Messiah himself is beyond the reach of satanic attack. So, subsequent to the ascension, Satan turns his attention to the **woman,** the followers of the Messiah.

God looks after the woman for 1,260 days, the same period of forty-two months or three and a half years mentioned in 11:2–3, 12:14, and 13:5. (For a full discussion, see under 11:2–3.) The 1,260 days cover the entire interadvental period. It begins immediately after Christ's ascension. It continues throughout the period of satanic assaults on the church, that is, the whole period until the Second Coming. During the entire period, God protects the church from satanic attacks. But the vision also applies with particular force to times of intense distress that may come when the church suffers violent attack. The protection comes in **the desert.** Israel, after the exodus from Egypt, wandered in the desert. This desert gave them relief from the idolatry and oppression of Egypt. But it was also a time of testing, when they were tempted to lose faith and rebel. They were to look forward to rest and satisfaction in the Promised Land. Similarly, the church looks forward to final rest in the new heaven and the new earth. But for now, she is subject to testing on earth.

The Dragon's Defeat (12:7–12)

The victory of Christ (12:5) results in sweeping consequences, beginning with the expulsion of Satan by Michael, who is functioning as an agent of Christ (see Dan. 10:21). We are not to think here of the fall of Satan at the time of creation, but of the defeat of Satan in the crucifixion and resurrection of Christ (Rev. 12:12; Col. 2:15; John 12:31).

The war was fought **in heaven.** The Bible indicates that until the time of Christ's triumph, Satan was permitted to appear in the heavenly places (Job 1:6; 2:1; Zech. 3:1–2; Luke 10:18). His abilities were curtailed by Christ's earthly ministry and above all by his resurrection and ascension (cf. Rev. 12:11).

As with the serpent in Genesis 3, Satan's chief weapon is his deceit. He **leads the whole world astray** (v. 9). He tries to confuse the church with heresies (v. 15), and he accuses people of sin before God (v. 10; Zech. 3:1–2).

In verses 10–12, **a loud voice in heaven,** the voice of heavenly worshipers, celebrates the fact that Christ has achieved the decisive victory. Satan has been defeated (vv. 7–9). His ability to accuse is curtailed (v. 10). The salvation and kingdom of God have already come (v. 10). However, strife still continues for a short time on earth (v. 12). As usual, this shortness is measured by prophetic standards, as in 1:3. The time for the fulfillment of God's purposes has arrived, and this fulfillment unfolds in a way that stretches out toward the consummation. Revelation reminds saints in distress that martyrdom may come, but that because of Christ's victory over death, the martyr is victorious rather than defeated by death (v. 11). Victory has both a present and a future manifestation.

Protection for the Woman (12:13–17)

Having failed to destroy Christ (12:4–5), the Dragon tries to destroy the people of Christ. He uses his mouth, representing his deceit (12:15, 9; 2 Thess. 2:9–10). When deceit fails, he persecutes the church (12:17–13:10). The woman flies to the desert—an image that speaks of the powerful care exercised by God on behalf of his people. His people receive powerful protection, even in very difficult circumstances. "For nothing is impossible with God" (Luke 1:37). By speaking of the desert and the period of three and a half years, Revelation here expands on the earlier summary in verse 6. The protection applies to the entire interadvental period (see the discussion under 12:6 and 11:2–3).

The earth comes to the help of the woman. The very structure of God's created world restricts and frustrates Satan's plans. Since he cannot wipe out the church as a whole through his deceit, he tries another plan: to **war against the rest of her offspring.** Chapter 13 shows that this war involves raising up earthly instruments of persecution.

The Beast (13:1–10)

A beast rising out of the sea represents persecuting power, especially the power of a demonized state. Its monstrous mixture of features shows its fierceness and repulsiveness. The Beast is hideous. One might be terrorized into submission, but who would genuinely want to worship this mass of ugliness? The rebellious world is fascinated with his power (13:4), but Christians have their eyes opened through this and other biblical revelations.

The Beast combines features from the four beasts of Daniel 7:1–8, 17–27. The beasts of Daniel represent idolatrous kingdoms. The Beast in Revelation must be a worldly kingdom summing up all of them. The state-controlled persecutions of Daniel and his friends thus suggest the nature of the persecution that the seven churches face from the Roman state—and the persecutions of later ages. Interpreters disagree about which particular persecution the Beast most directly represents (see "Schools of Interpretation" in the Introduction). Because it expresses a general principle of satanic opposition, we may expect multiple manifestations. As indicated in the Introduction, these manifestations occurred in the first century, will occur in the final crisis, and have been occurring at all times in between.

In Asia Minor, local officials threatened to kill Christians if they refused to worship the Roman emperor. A similar opposition to godly worship will crop up just before the Second Coming (2 Thess. 2:4). Persecutions come sporadically in between these two times (2 Tim. 3:12–13; 1 Peter 4:12–19; Matt. 24:9). Second Thessalonians 2:7–8 indicates that we are dealing with a repeated pattern of satanic opposition ("the secret power of lawlessness"). This lawlessness is currently restrained, but will have a final, climactic outbreak ("and then the lawless one will be revealed"). Christians must not be surprised by these pressures. They must face martyrdom, if necessary, knowing that God is in control and that his triumph is certain.

The Beast represents in the first place demonized state power that demands worship. As with Shadrach, Meshach, and Abednego (Dan. 3), the demonized state threatens to kill Christians unless they bow down. But the symbolism of the Beast applies also to more subtle temptations to idolatry. In democratic countries, the state does not insist on literal worship. But citizens are tempted to look to the state as if it were a messiah. It is the greatest concentration of earthly power, and so it must be the remedy for all ills—economic, social, medical, moral, and even spiritual. Moreover, blatant state persecution threatens to overwhelm us through fear. But in subtle ways we are tempted to give ultimate commitments to anything that we fear: fear of man (human opinion), fear of death, fear of pain, fear of poverty. So this picture of idolatry has universal application (see "Counterfeiting" in the Introduction).

The Beast is a counterfeit of Christ. Note the following parallels:

- The Beast is an image of Satan, who brought him forth (13:1), just as Christ is the exact image of God, begotten by the Father (Col. 1:15; Heb. 1:3; Ps. 2:7).

- The Beast has ten crowns, while Christ has many crowns (19:12).
- The Beast has blasphemous names written on him, while Christ has worthy names (19:12).
- The Dragon has given the Beast his power, his throne, and great authority (13:2), just as Christ has power (5:12–13), a throne (3:21), and authority (12:10) from the Father (John 5:21–23).
- The Beast has a healed fatal wound, counterfeiting Christ's resurrection (13:3). The Beast's healing is one of the principal features that attracts followers, just as the resurrection of Christ is one of the principal points of evangelistic proclamation.
- Worship is directed both to the Dragon and to the Beast, just as Christians worship both the Father and the Son (John 5:23).
- The Beast attracts the worship of the whole world (13:3), just as Christ is to be worshiped universally.
- The Beast utters blasphemies, while Christ utters the praises of God (Heb. 2:12).
- The Beast makes war against the saints, while Christ makes war against the Beast (19:11–21). The song of praise to the Beast in 13:4 counterfeits the song to God, the warrior, in Exodus 15:11. The striking juxtaposition of Christ and the Beast in 19:11–21 shows that they are the two main warriors in the battle. Christ is the divine warrior, fulfilling the imagery of Exodus 15:3; Isaiah 59:16–18; 63:1–6; Habakkuk 3:3–15; Zechariah 9:13–15; 14:1–5. The Beast is the unholy, counterfeit warrior, fulfilling the imagery of Daniel 7:1–8.

Satan himself attempts to counterfeit God the Father. He engages in a mock creation, in which he brings forth his image out of chaotic waters (13:1; cf. Gen. 1:2). Similarly, the False Prophet, or the beast from the earth (13:11–18), counterfeits the work of the Holy Spirit. He desires that people worship not himself, but the Beast, just as the Holy Spirit glorifies Christ (John 16:14). He works miraculous signs, counterfeiting the miracles of the Holy Spirit (13:13–14). He forces a mark on his subjects (13:16), just as Christians are sealed with the Holy Spirit (Eph. 1:13).

Together, Satan, the Beast, and the False Prophet form an unholy trio (16:13). They counterfeit the Holy Trinity (see "Counterfeiting" in the Introduction). Satan, as a deceiver, is always trying to make his ways look attractive (2 Cor. 11:14–15). Our danger lies in the fact that his counterfeits are always close to the real thing, and we may mistake the one for the other. But when Revelation opens our eyes, there is a world of difference between his horrors and God's beauties. We can be confident because he is only a counterfeiter, an imitator, not a creator. And his productions are always bestial and degenerate like himself. Beasts must give way before Christ the king (19:11–21).

One final counterfeit figure exists, namely Babylon the prostitute, the counterfeit of the bride of Christ (see 17:1–19:10).

The Beast's **ten horns** imitate the ten horns of the Dragon (12:3). They represent his power. They take particular form in "ten kings" who help execute his purpose (17:12). They correspond to the ten horns of the fourth beast in Daniel 7:7, 20. The **seven heads** represent multiple manifestations, as in 17:10, again imitating the Dragon (12:3). The Beast combines features of a leopard, a bear, and a lion (v. 2). He sums up the beasts in Daniel 7:2–7, and is more fierce and hideous than any of them.

Behind the Beast, a perversion of state power, stands the Dragon, who energizes and endorses him (v. 2). Christians are to be alert to satanic influence, not only with individuals, but also with institutions and whole societies. The mass of people in the Roman Empire were attracted to emperor worship, but the number of people seduced did not lessen the seriousness of their error. Likewise, communism, fascism, Hinduism, materialism, and New Age spirituality may be mass movements today, but Christians must resist them.

The Beast's **mortal wound** and his recovery counterfeit Christ's resurrection. Revelation may be alluding to a myth that grew up after Nero's death in A.D. 68. A rumor spread that he had not really died, and that he would soon return at the head of the Parthians to wreak vengeance. But the symbolism has broader application. The revival of a powerful movement or an institution after serious trouble seems to indicate to its followers that it is invincible. The Empire seemed to survive all threats, thereby showing that it was eternal and attracting more worship than ever. But all such hopes are mistaken. Only Christ brings eternal life, and only his kingdom will last forever.

The Beast's counterfeit character comes out clearly in his blasphemies (v. 5). Even these are ultimately under God's control, as is implied by the phrase **was given.** God gives people even the breath through which they blaspheme him. The sovereignty of God underlines the security of the saints and the ultimate futility of all opposition to God.

In addition, we find that the Beast's power has a definite limit. He exercises his authority for **forty-two months.** This period is the same period of distress and persecution mentioned in 11:2–3; 12:6, 14 (see the discussion at 11:2).

The Beast compels worship (13:8), and when the saints refuse to submit, they are martyred. But despite their apparent defeat, martyrs enjoy victory with Christ both immediately (6:9–11) and when their prayers for the final defeat of the Beast are answered (19:11–21). The Beast aspires to universal control and allegiance from **every tribe, people, language and nation** (v. 7). But ultimately all nations belong to Christ (5:9). The necessity for decision is set out in black and white. One must give ultimate allegiance either to Christ or to the Beast. One cannot be neutral. All except the saints go after the Beast, since, apart from Christ, people remain in the power of Satan and darkness (Col. 1:13; Eph. 2:1–3; Gal. 1:4; Acts 4:12).

The book of life (13:8) is the heavenly roster of those destined to new life through the blood of Christ (5:9; see 3:5). As in 17:8, the phrase "from the creation of the world" modifies not "slain" but "written." The names of the saints, then, were "written before the foundation of the world in the book of life of the Lamb that was slain." In the midst of persecution and the immense power of the Beast, the saints may find security in God's guarantee of their heavenly citizenship. Similar guarantees are found in 7:1–17; 17:8; 20:12, 15; 21:27.

The exhortation to hear (v. 9) picks up on earlier exhortation in 2:7, 11, 17, 29; 3:6, 13, 22—and Jesus' exhortations in Matthew 11:15; 13:9, 43; Mark 4:9, 23; 8:18; Luke 8:8; 14:35; cf. Matthew 7:24, 26. The saints must take to heart the warning of Revelation, and be on the alert to resist the deceptions of the Beast as well as his threats and intimidation.

Patient endurance (v. 10), believing in God's faithfulness and his triumph through Christ, enables the saints to pass through all distresses. God never promises that we will be free from suffering in this world; on the contrary, he repeatedly announces that it will come. But he promises sustenance. "In this world you will have trouble. But take heart! I have overcome the world" (John 16:33) (see 1:9).

The False Prophet (13:11–18)

The beast from the earth, also called the False Prophet (16:13; 19:20; 20:10), functions as a propagandist for the Beast. His actions counterfeit the witness of the Holy Spirit (see "Counterfeiting" in the Introduction).

In first-century Asia Minor, the main propagandists were priests of the emperor cult and the "Commune of Asia," a council of distinguished city representatives who promoted loyalty to the emperor. In our day as well, totalitarianism enlists propagandists. Just before the Second Coming, counterfeit miracles will accompany the appearance of the lawless one (2 Thess. 2:9). The False Prophet embodies a repeatable pattern (see "Schools of Interpretation" in the Introduction). Satan uses deceit as his main weapon (Rev. 12:9; 20:3). He uses human instruments and institutions to magnify and propagate his deceits.

What, then, are the principal means of deceit around us now? In our modern society, the mass media, educational institutions, advertising, and the whole "knowledge industry" offer the principal channels through which people learn and confirm their views of themselves and their world. In principle, technologically enhanced communication and social organizations can support either truth or error, righteousness or wickedness. But in societies affected by the Fall, all too often distortions of the truth invite people to pursue idols and simultaneously blind them to the realities of their idolatry. For example, the media may become filled with the presuppositions of a materialistic worldview. In the resulting message, God need not be mentioned except in expletives, since he is nonexistent, absent, or irrelevant. Humanity invents its own meanings. We are part of an evolutionary whole. Progress comes by freeing ourselves from a primitive past. Money, health, intelligence, beauty, and sexual pleasure give us the good life. And so Herbert Schlossberg (*Idols for Destruction*) finds himself attacking modern idols called "history," "humanity," "mammon," "nature," "power," and even "religion," which inhabit our knowledge industry and float through its channels of communication.

These ideas pervade the atmosphere. They are all the more insidious because they are "atmospheric." They tend to be assumed rather than argued. One receives the subtle impression that it is all obvious. Everyone who is informed, everyone who is "with it," has gone past the stage of questioning. In reality, though, there never was a fundamental questioning, because the ideas seem so natural and inevitable. The average person is no more aware of them than the fish is aware of the water in which it has swum since its birth. The few who are aware can still take comfort. They may say to themselves, "How could we possibly be wrong, when the miracles of modern science and technology show the superiority of our ideas over those of the past?"

Technology, then, becomes the worker of miraculous signs (13:14). The signs tells us that true power resides in the modern view of the world. Worship the power of the Beast, the power of technocratic state organization, the power of the expert, because technology can work wonders like no one else.

The second beast is from the earth (v. 11), whereas the first is from the sea (v. 1). Together, then, they hint at the attempt to master the whole earth, both sea and dry land. Interestingly, these two beasts are modeled after the two monsters in Job 40:15–41:34. The behemoth exercises power on land (Job 40:15–24), and the leviathan on water (Job 41:1–34). The ancient Near East produced multiple speculations about a land monster and a sea monster. Some Jews thought that the two monsters were now hidden, but would appear in the last days and be destroyed. Job is probably referring to the hippopotamus and the crocodile, but with incredibly charged, hyperbolic, poetic imagery. Readers are invited to use these creatures as windows on the terrors of nightmares and the preternatural realm of demons. In Job, God is the Creator and therefore the master of them all. So is he also in Revelation, where the pairing of the two beasts increases the sense of their power and terror: they are superhuman, cosmic, ageless monsters. But Revelation, like Job, simultaneously proclaims that God has bounded them from the beginning.

The second beast has **two horns like a lamb** (v. 11). Like the first beast, he offers counterfeiting. When he exercises the authority of the first beast (v. 12), he is counterfeiting Jesus' sending of the Holy Spirit as "another Counselor" with his authority (John 16:13–15). He promotes worship of the Beast (Rev. 13:12), just as the Holy Spirit promotes worship of Christ. He performs miraculous signs (v. 13), analogous to the Spirit-wrought signs in the book of Acts. Priests in the first century were not above working a little fakery to encourage people to come and patronize their temples. In the first century, the image (v. 14) is the image of the emperor set up in the local temple dedicated to the imperial cult. Now it is the concrete thing through which godlike power and presence is mediated and adored: for some people, the TV set!

All who refused to worship the image were **to be killed** (v. 15). Nebuchadnezzar threatened death to Shadrach, Meshach, and Abednego for not bowing down to his image (Dan. 3). Christians in the Roman Empire might be executed for treason, or disloyalty to the emperor, if they refused to participate in the imperial cult. Totalitarian governments in our time are seldom so crude. But the local government official, as an image of government power, requires total allegiance such as a Christian cannot give.

Successful modern democratic governments are not literally killing people. They do not need to, as long as their idolatrous programs are so successful! They tend not toward paternal severity, but toward maternal smothering. The state undertakes to help you by stuffing you with what is good for you, according to its supposedly enlightened, beneficent judgment. And if you do not agree, you are socially unfit and maladapted. The old "you" must be "killed," socially speaking, by social engineering, in order that the new "you" may function as a upstanding, healthy citizen of the state. To this end, the state uses education, financial penalties, financial inducements, endless regulations, and bureaucrats overseeing and directing your decisions. No, we Christians in such a country do not feel the immediate threat of the sword. But untangling ourselves from the clinging web of idolatry is like death. For the web exists inside us as well as outside, in the ways in which we have already, as members of our society, absorbed its godless assumptions. As verse 16 indicates, participation in society is hardly possible without idolatry. Society regards the Christian as a misfit, a misanthrope, a victim of insanity. The Christian does not accept the "obvious verities," and so cannot be trusted. Thus, a consistent Christian will find it difficult to fit in and mix with pagan society. The difficulties may be subtle, as in "tolerant" modern democratic societies, or they may be blatant and harsh, as in the Roman Empire or modern totalitarian countries, where Christians may suffer the confiscation of their property.

What is **the mark** (vv. 16–17) of the Beast? It is a counterfeit for the seal of God's name on the saints (7:2–8; 14:1; cf. Ezek. 9; Deut. 6:8). The Beast owns those who are marked, and they are his slaves (14:9; 19:20; 20:4). A mark denotes spiritual allegiance and ownership, both in the case of God's mark and in the case of the Beast's counterfeit mark. In both cases, the mark is at root spiritual rather than visible. The multitude of speculations about a visible mark are beside the point.

What about the number 666? Divine completeness would be expressed by 777, and 666 consistently falls short of that. Thus, the number 666 has an obvious symbolic value. But there may be a further association. In both Hebrew and Greek, a numerical value was associated with each letter of the alphabet. In Greek, A had the value of 1, B had the value of 2, I had the value of 10, and so on. The letters were sometimes used as a shorthand for numbers. Both Jews and pagans sometimes played arithmetical games with the numerical value of whole words. Christians found that the name Jesus had the numerical value of 888 in Greek. Hence, the number 666 contrasts with the name of Jesus (cf. 14:1). Jesus is the Christ, who brings in the new creation on the eighth day. The Beast is the Antichrist, who counterfeits Christ, but falls short.

Many have attempted to connect the number 666 with the numerical value of someone's name. But there are far too many possibilities. Some people have transliterated or translated names into Hebrew or Greek, as well as putting them in a Roman alphabet; others have used different forms of names, adding or deleting titles and abbreviations of titles and names. By such means, people have succeeded in correlating the number with each of the main Roman emperors of the time—Nero, Vespasian, Titus, and Domitian—and with modern tyrannical figures. But

such speculations miss the point. Revelation calls not for cleverness, but for spiritual discernment.[21]

The 144,000 (14:1–5)

The 144,000 represent the saints in their complete number
(see 7:4–8). They form a priestly company (5:10), consecrated
to offer praise to God on the holy mount. God affirms his ownership and protection by placing his mark on them, in contrast to
the mark of the Beast in 13:16–18. The **sound from heaven** is
probably the sound of praise from the saints. Their loudness and
exuberance reflect the loud thunder of God himself when he appears in theophany, as at Mount Sinai (Ex. 19:16; Ezek. 1:24;
Rev. 1:10; 4:5). The **new song** (v. 3) picks up the Old Testament
theme of singing new songs to celebrate new days of victory for
God (Pss. 33:3; 40:3; 96:1; 98:1; 144:9; 149:1). **No one could
learn the song** except the 144,000, that is, the redeemed. The
144,000 symbolize all the people of God, every one of whom is
known and numbered by God. The inhabitants of earth who
have not been redeemed cannot participate. The experience of,
and participation in, God's salvation give us a special inner ap-
preciation of his goodness, greatness, and grace.

The 144,000 are described as **chaste.** Sexual imagery is used
here to denote spiritual purity. Christ's faithful followers keep
away from Babylon the prostitute and are loyal to him exclusively, as his pure bride (19:7–8; Eph. 5:26–27). Sexual purity
is of course one element in spiritual purity (1 Cor. 6:15–20).

Three Angelic Proclaimers (14:6–11)

Now come three announcements from three angelic beings.
Because of their similarity in pattern, these three episodes belong together as a single symbolic history (14:6–11). This symbolic history is the sixth out of seven (see "Structure" in the
Introduction). The seventh symbolic history includes the appearing of the Son of Man (14:14), that is, the Second Coming.
Thematically, angels are placed just before this event to give a

final warning that judgment is coming on all those who have not repented.

God may of course send extraordinary warnings just before and during the final crisis leading to the Second Coming. But the message has a point throughout the church age. Through the preaching of the church, the Lord gives warning to the unrepentant world.

The first angel calls on everyone to repent (14:6–7)—those in **every nation, tribe, language and people.** As this message reaches all nations, the promise made to Abraham that all peoples would be blessed is fulfilled (Gen. 12:3). But curse also comes to those who curse Abraham, and now, in the last days, this curse falls on those who do not repent in response to the gospel. As other parts of Revelation make clear, the gospel involves turning to Christ. But here the focus is on worshiping and fearing God. The chief sin of the nations is their refusal to worship the One who has created and sustained them (Rom. 1:18–32; Acts 14:15–17; 17:22–31). The coming of the gospel is not what creates guilt; people are already guilty for rebelling against God. The gospel shows the way of escape by returning to God before it is too late, for **the hour of his judgment has come** (v. 7). The usual three parts of the universe—heaven, dry land, and sea—become four parts when one distinguishes salt water from fresh water. These four parts of the universe receive judgments in the first four trumpets (8:7–12) and the first four bowls (16:1–9). The mention of the four parts here (v. 7) thus contains a subtle reminder of the fierceness of God's judgment against rebels.

The second angel announces the fall of Babylon, who seduced the nations. The center of false worship has fallen (see the further development of this theme in chapters 17–18). The message is, in effect, "Turn to true worship before it is too late." **Babylon the Great,** the great seductress, is further described in 17:1–19:10. She seduces people to commit **adulteries.** Sexual immorality, like idolatry (which is spiritual adultery), was a ma-

jor temptation for the seven churches (see 2:20). Its effect, like
that of drunkenness, is confusion of mind, shame, foolishness,
and disgrace (see 17:2, 4; 18:3; 19:2; Jer. 51:7; Prov. 9:13–18).

The third angel elaborates on the fearsome judgment that
comes upon the unrepentant, the followers of the Beast. This
threat is simultaneously an encouragement to the saints. It encourages them to hold fast, even under intense suffering. Their
suffering is but little in comparison with the wrath of God. It
also shows that ultimate vindication will come. The Christian
faith, which seems so small and puny to the world, will be shown
to be true, and the worshipers of the Beast, who seem so secure
because of the worldly might of the Roman Empire, will find all
their false hopes come to nothing.

Those who worship the Beast **will be tormented with
burning sulfur** (v. 10). The torment goes on forever: not only
does the smoke rise forever, but the sufferers have no rest, no
sabbath, no relief (v. 11). What do we do with this picture?

The idea of endless torment is abhorrent to modern Western
sensibilities. It troubles many Christians as well as non-
Christians, and has caused not a few in our day to look for some
escape from the apparent meaning of these verses. Let us consider this matter carefully. The Christian ideal of love, which has
had a leavening effect on the West, has sensitized us to the appalling nature of cruelty and torture. Ancient pagan societies,
before the coming of Christianity, were shockingly brutal to their
enemies, and too few within them had much of a troubled con-
science. How did Christianity change this situation? It showed
that such cruelty is heinous because people are made in the image of God—and they are or may become our brothers and sis-
ters in Christ. Secularization converted this love for one's neigh-
bor into a wishy-washy sentimentality. It liked to imagine that
everybody is innocent and that suffering is senseless. Thus, we
have to separate between what is good and what is bad in modern attitudes. We must purify our hearts and beware of the influence of modern distortions of biblical truth.

Moreover, the Second Coming represents a radical change in the situation, in that the possibility of repentance comes to an end. We quite rightly train ourselves during this age to have a hopeful attitude toward even the most terrible sinner. We pray and hope for repentance. We learn to love our enemies. This viewpoint is appropriate during this age, but it does not fit the arena of the Second Coming. Moreover, during the present age we love and admire many things about pagans because, even in their rebellion, they display many admirable reflections of God's goodness. Our admiration may be proper now, but that will change when we see undiluted wickedness in all its ugliness and hideousness. The Second Coming brings about a separation between good and evil. This means not only a separation of good people from evil people, but a separation between good and evil within people. Within evil people, evil will come to full fruition. Goodness will remain only with God and those enjoying his blessing. It is hard for us to picture just how bad evil may actually become.

We must let God be God. He knows what he is doing when he displays mercy and when he displays justice. We must therefore take the teaching in Revelation seriously. We must reckon with the fact that God is indeed a God of justice and of punishment for evil. Only by repenting and turning to Christ can one escape from hell.

(On the Beast and his mark, see 13:1–10 and 13:16.)

Interlude: Relief for the Saints (14:12–13)

In the midst of these threats of judgment comes a message to the saints: persevere (see 1:9). Do not cave in to the temptations of the surrounding society and its idolatries, however powerful and seductive they may appear. Your reward will yet come (v. 13). Unlike the worshipers of the Beast, you will have rest.

The Appearing of One Like a Son of Man (14:14–20)

The section 14:14–20 is the last of the seven symbolic histories. It depicts the Second Coming as the harvest over which the

Son of Man presides (cf. Matt. 13:36–43; Joel 3:12–16). The "one 'like a son of man'" is Jesus Christ (1:13; Dan. 7:13–14).

Two harvests are described, one of grain (14:14–16) and one of grapes (14:17–20). These are perhaps two aspects of the same judgment. Alternatively, the grain harvest may be the harvest of the righteous (Luke 3:17), followed by the harvest of the wicked in 14:17–20. The main background is the picture of the final divine harvest in Joel 3:12–16. In Joel, grain is harvested with a sickle, and grapes are trampled in the winepress; both carry the primary connotation of punishment. But in Revelation, specific connotations of punishment come only with the grape harvest, when grapes are thrown into **the great winepress of God's wrath** (v. 19). The grain harvest may symbolize the harvest of the righteous (as in 14:1–5). More likely, however, the passage in Joel gives us the main clue to interpretation. Both harvests are primarily about the judging of the wicked. As in Joel, deliverance for God's people is symbolized in other ways, but it still comes in conjunction with the judgment of the wicked.

The Seven Bowls (15:1–16:21)

The cycle of seven bowls of God's wrath constitutes the fourth cycle of visions leading up to the Second Coming (see "Structure" in the Introduction). The opening scene of worship (15:1–16:1) calls to mind the worship around God's throne in 4:1–5:14. The overcomers rejoice in God's presence (15:2). Seven resplendent angels receive bowls from the presence of God in the temple. The bowls symbolize the cup of God's wrath, which in the Old Testament makes the nations drunk (cf. Isa. 51:17, 20, 22; Jer. 25:15–29; Lam. 4:21; Ezek. 23:31–34; Hab. 2:16; Rev. 14:10; 16:19). The bowls are poured out at God's command (16:1), resulting in seven last plagues. The plagues lead up to and include the Second Coming, since "with them God's wrath is completed" (15:1).

The seven bowls show notable similarities to the seven trumpets. The first four bowls, like the first four trumpets, result in devastation on the four major regions of the world: dry land, sea, fresh water, and sky. Like the trumpets, the bowls are reminiscent of the Mosaic plagues against Egypt. But the bowls result in more severe judgments than did the trumpets. The trumpet judgments typically affected a third of the area, but the bowls affect the whole.

These bowls symbolize the judgments of God against evildoers. The general pattern may include both the judgments against the godless Roman Empire and the final crisis leading up to the Second Coming (see "Schools of Interpretation" in the

Introduction). The symbolism also asserts that, throughout this age, God may at his pleasure send judgments of utmost devastation on those who rebel against him.

The Origin of the Bowls in God and His Worship (15:1–8)

As we progress through the book of Revelation, the visions focus more and more on the climactic judgments of the Second Coming. The judgments of the seven bowls remind us of the nearness of the last things, not only by speaking of **the seven last plagues,** but by stating that **with them God's wrath is completed.**

The events unfold beside **a sea of glass mixed with fire** (v. 2). The sea is the same as the one in 4:6. We see the events as issuing from God's presence and his throne. Terrible disasters do not come by accident, but according to the just judgment of God. They are harbingers of the final judgment of the Second Coming. As in 4:6, the sea is reminiscent not only of the crossing of the Red Sea, but also of God's power to subdue the chaos of the sea. The Israelites stood on the far shore of the Red Sea and observed the death of their enemies through God's power. In the last days, victorious saints likewise stand on the far side of their troubles and the persecutions of the Beast. As in 14:3, they take up a new song of victory. It repeats the old **song of Moses,** in that God's final victory repeats the earlier victory at the Red Sea (see Ex. 15). The plagues that follow in Revelation 16 are reminiscent of the plagues that came on Egypt.

The saints praise God for the greatness and awesomeness of his power, but also for his justice in these powerful, miraculous acts (v. 3). God's acts of judgment are never arbitrary or spiteful, but just payment for evil deeds (cf. 15:4; 16:5, 7; 19:2, 11; see also 14:10–12).

When God manifests his greatness in his deeds, people from all nations see who he is. They may nevertheless continue unrepentant, as the Egyptians did during the plagues on their land.

But there may also be a favorable response. Nations formerly in the darkness of paganism see the light of God's revelation (Isa. 60:1–3). The coming of **all nations,** fulfilled in 21:24–26, fulfills the promise given to Abraham (Gen. 12:3).

In verses 5–8 the vision now shifts to **the temple.** Old Testament images of the tabernacle, the altar, the temple, God's throne, clouds, fire, and thunder all converge in Revelation to represent in various ways the presence of God in his splendor, might, and beauty (see on 4:1–5:14). The bowls are moved from the temple area into the hands of the angels who will pour them out. This indicates again that God originates the judgments that come upon men.

The angels are **dressed in clean, shining linen** (v. 6), which is Old Testament priestly clothing (Ex. 28:42; Lev. 16:4). The holiness of God's judgments is thereby emphasized (see 15:3–4). The four living creatures refer us back to 4:6.

Smoke (v. 8) or thick cloud frequently accompanies God's presence, especially when he is angry. The associations include Mount Sinai (Ex. 19:9, 16, 18; 20:18) and the visions of Isaiah and Ezekiel (Isa. 6:4; Ezek. 1:4; cf. Num. 12:5; Pss. 18:8, 11; 74:1).

Pouring Out the First Four Bowls (16:1–9)

Now the bowls begin to be poured out. **A loud voice** comes from the temple (v. 1), indicating that the events take place according to God's instructions and plan.

The first angel pours his bowl **on the earth** (the land), the first of the four major regions of the universe. The plagues fall not on all human beings, but on the ungodly: **the people who had the mark of the beast and worshiped his image** (v. 2). (On the image of the Beast, see 13:14–15.) The sores are like the Egyptian plague of boils (Ex. 9:8–12).

The second plague is like the Egyptian plague of blood (Ex. 7:14–24).

With the third plague, God's true servants praise him for his justice, taking up the theme of 15:3. As with the *lex talionis* (Ex.

21:24; Lev. 24:20; Deut. 19:21; Pss. 7:16; 9:15–16; Obad. 15; Matt. 7:1–2), the punishment fits the crime.

The fourth plague (vv. 8–9), scorching with fire, corresponds to the judgment by fire prophesied in the Old Testament (e.g., Joel 2:3; Isa. 66:15; Mal. 4:1–2). Despite the severity of their suffering, people refuse to repent (vv. 9, 11). This vision represents people in the hardness of their heart. Rather than taking the warning to heart, they use it as an occasion to be angry with God.

Pouring Out the Last Bowls (16:10–21)

The fifth plague is like the Egyptian plague of darkness (Ex. 10:21–23). The repeated refusal to repent (cf. v. 9) prepares us for the last two plagues. In their rage, people attempt a direct assault on God (the sixth plague), and God puts down their rebellion for good (the seventh plague).

The sixth plague (vv. 12–16) shows the preparations for the final battle, the battle of Armageddon. Aspects of this same battle have already been described in one way or another: the kings and all kinds of people cluster together in 6:15; the army beyond the Euphrates is summoned in 9:14; the Beast fights against the saints in 11:7 and 13:1–10. Further descriptions occur in 17:13–14; 19:11–21; 20:7–10. The later passages describe the battle with increasing detail and precision, all based on the eschatological battle of Gog and Magog in Ezekiel 38–39. Throughout the church age, there have been intense confrontations between God and the forces of Satan (cf. 2:10, 13), but the most intense one comes at the Second Coming (19:11–21).

Not all interpreters agree that these various passages describe the same battle. But once we appreciate the thematic concerns of Revelation, and the pattern of seven cycles all leading up to the Second Coming, the thematic unity of the various passages becomes a strong pointer to their inward unity. After all, how many *last* battles can there be, **on the great day of God Almighty** (16:14; cf. 6:16–17; 15:1!)?

The Euphrates river dries up to allow for the movement of great armies, as in 9:14. The Dragon, the Beast, and the False Prophet appear together (v. 13). The False Prophet is the same as the beast from the earth in 13:11–18. The three together form a counterfeit of the Holy Trinity (see "Counterfeiting" in the Introduction). Not only are they demonic in their own right, but, at this climactic point, they become generators of further demonic spirits, in the form of frogs. They perform miraculous signs, as in 2 Thessalonians 2:9–10 and Revelation 13:13–15, to deceive the reprobate. These people are all too willing to be deceived because they have already rejected God's truth (2 Thess. 2:10–11; John 3:18–20).

They **gather them for the battle.** In the climactic battle, all the forces of wickedness are assembled to make war against the warrior Lamb (17:14). This final battle reminds us of the battle between God and Pharaoh in Exodus 15:2, but the panorama is cosmic in scope. In Hebrew, **Armageddon** means "mount of Megiddo." In ancient Israel, Megiddo was a key city along a major route between the great kingdoms of Mesopotamia and Egypt. Huge armies could assemble in the neighboring plain of Esdraelon. Moreover, God's people had experienced decisive battles there (Judg. 5:19; 2 Chron. 35:20–22). Thus, it is a fitting symbol for the location of the climactic battle.

The name is symbolic, and so it cannot be used as a basis for speculations about the geographical details of the final battle. In any case, the final battle is preeminently spiritual in character. Attempts to correlate it with the maneuvers of particular national armies miss the point. The battle is between the servants of God and the enemies of God, not between two nations of the world. Because of the missionary expansion of the church, nearly all nations now have in their midst both Christians and non-Christians.

The seventh bowl (vv. 17–21) brings the cycle of judgments to an end. Like the other cycles, this one ends with the Second Coming (see "Structure" in the Introduction), though the symbols of the Second Coming are not as obvious as in some other cases. Note that 15:1 has already indicated that the end of the wrath of God would come with the seventh bowl. The removal of all islands and mountains in 16:20 corresponds to the final shaking of the earth in 6:14 and 20:11 (cf. Heb. 12:26–27). Elsewhere, the fall of Babylon is immediately followed by the marriage supper of the Lamb (19:1–10). In 17:14–17, the fall of Babylon is immediately associated with the final battle, which takes place at the Second Coming (19:11–21). Moreover, the final battle was imminent in 16:16. Finally, in Revelation the imagery of the final battle is repeatedly drawn from Ezekiel 38–39 (see the note on 16:14). This passage (16:17–21) fits into this pattern by grouping together an earthquake, the overturning of mountains, and hail, as in Ezekiel 38:19–23. Hence, it describes the divine plagues or judgments accompanying the battle. A description of other aspects of the battle is delayed until 19:11–21, in keeping with the dramatic plan of Revelation.

Babylon the Prostitute (17:1–19:10)

In the fifth major cycle of judgments, 17:1–19:10, Babylon the prostitute appears, representing the seductions of the world (17:4; 18:3). The destruction of Babylon goes together thematically with the destruction of the other primary agents of wickedness. We see the destruction of the Beast and the False Prophet in 19:11–21 and the destruction of Satan in 20:7–10. It is best to see these three destructive, judgmental episodes as being thematically parallel rather than occurring in strict chronological succession. Together they make up the final three of Revelation's seven cycles of judgment (see "Structure" in the Introduction).

The corruptions of Babylon contrast with the purity of the bride of the Lamb (19:7–9). Babylon sums up in herself the worship of the godless world. By contrast, the bride (the church) represents the worshipers of the true God. Just as Satan, the Beast, and the False Prophet form a counterfeit Trinity, Babylon is a counterfeit church, seducing the world to give its allegiance to the counterfeit Trinity (see "Counterfeiting" in the Introduction).

The seven messages of judgment on Babylon consist of three angelic messages of doom (17:7–18; 18:1–3; 18:4–8), three laments by those committed to Babylon (18:9–10; 18:11–17a; 18:17b–19, plus a command from heaven to rejoice in 18:20), and a climactic pronouncement of the permanence of her fall

(18:21–24) (fig. 19; see also "Rhetorical Structure" under "Structure" in the Introduction).

Fig. 19. Messages of Judgment on Babylon

Passage	Speaker	Message
17:7–18	angel (with bowl)	fall of Beast and Babylon
18:1–3	bright angel with authority	fall of Babylon
18:4–8	voice from heaven	come out from Babylon
18:9–10	kings of the earth	lament
18:11–17a	merchants of the earth	lament
18:17b–19	sailors	lament
18:20	voice from heaven	rejoice
18:21–24	a mighty angel	permanent fall of Babylon

Satan attacks the saints in two main ways. The Beast attacks with power and persecution, endeavoring to destroy the witness of the saints and force them to worship the Beast. Babylon attacks with seduction, endeavoring to destroy the purity of the saints (fig. 20).

Fig. 20. Two Kinds of Satanic Opposition

• The Beast	• Persecuting power
• The Prostitute	• Seductive luxury

Babylon stands for the city of Rome with its immorality. For the seven churches of Revelation, Rome was the source of all manner of idolatry—not only the worship of the Roman emperor, but the structures of an idolatrous society. The paganism of the cities of Asia Minor made each one a small manifestation of Babylon. Full economic and social participation in city life (13:17) involved attendance at idolatrous feasts and pagan religious celebrations. Babylon is attractive because she promises the pleasures of sensuality and prosperity. Both the clothing of Babylon in 17:4 and the laments in 18:9–20 indicate that much of the attraction of Babylon lies in her wealth and luxury. The pagans in Asia looked to Rome as the source and guarantee of economic well-being and material comfort. They gave political allegiance and worship to the Roman emperor, not only because they feared the power of Rome, but because they loved the economic benefits that they received from her.

Worship of the emperor was expected as an expression of political allegiance. Pagans called Christians atheists because they did not worship the many gods recognized by Greco-Roman religion, and called them haters of mankind because they withdrew from compromised forms of social life (cf. 1 Peter 4:3–4; 2:12). In reaction to this pressure, even some professing Christians argued that participation in idolatrous feasts and sexual immorality were acceptable (Rev. 2:14, 20; cf. 1 Cor. 6:12–20). The woman called Jezebel in Revelation 2:20–23 was a key seducer, whose work is generalized and more deeply symbolized as Babylon the prostitute (compare 2:21–22 with 17:2).

The cities of the first century have not been the only centers of idolatry, greed, materialism, and sexual immorality. Our modern cities, with their wealth, false religions, and sexual exploitation, are modern forms of Babylon. The media and their advertisements can bring into our homes and thoughts the seductions of money, sex, power, and pleasure. Advertisements tell us that satisfaction and meaningful living can be found if only we buy the latest product. They say, "If only you have enough money and toys and sensual pleasures, you will be fulfilled." Thus, the symbolism of Babylon is capable of multiple embodiments, including a final, climactic embodiment just before the Second Coming (see "Schools of Interpretation" in the Introduction).

Little babylons also operate in the recesses of our heart (fig. 21). The Beast controls his subjects through fear; the Prostitute seduces people by playing on their lusts with the enticements of illicit pleasures. However subtle the remaining sinful tendencies in the Christian's heart may be, they also involve fear and lust. We capitulate and compromise with sin because of either fear or lust. We are afraid of suffering and shame. Or we lust after the desires of our heart. Sex, wealth, fame, power, health, and beauty can all be objects of our lust.

FIG. 21. IDOLATRIES OF THE HEART

The Sway of the Beast	The Sway of the Prostitute
• fear	• lustful desire
• passive, retreating	• active, advancing
• avoid pain	• get pleasure
• at any cost	• at any cost
• for *me*	• for *me*

But how foolish it all is! It will all come to nothing, because of God's judgment (fig. 22). But it is nothing even now, because it means forsaking God, who is the true object of proper fear and proper desire. In the new Jerusalem, God grants the pleasure of the marriage supper of the Lamb, the wealth of streets paved with gold, the fame of being known by God and having his name on one's forehead, the power of the throne, the health of no sickness or death, and the beauty of the new city's architecture. The objects of our lust are only tawdry counterfeits of what God has created out of his own bounty and what he will bestow in unfathomable fullness.

FIG. 22. THE DESTRUCTION OF IDOLS

God judges idols (15:1).	God ⟹ Beast
Idols destroy idolaters (17:16–17)	Beast ⟹ Prostitute

Much of the imagery in this passage about the Prostitute accurately describes Jerusalem before its destruction. In refusing to accept the Messiah, she became a prostitute, as she had in the Old Testament (Luke 21:9–18; 11:47–51; Isa. 1:21; Ezek. 16;

23; Hos. 2). Revelation 11:8 links Jerusalem with Sodom and Egypt. A few interpreters have therefore argued in favor of identifying Babylon the prostitute with Jerusalem. But Jerusalem was only one instance of a society seducing people away from true worship. Ancient Babylon and Tyre were other examples, and Revelation accordingly takes up the language of the Old Testament prophetic condemnations of Babylon and Tyre (Jer. 50–51; Ezek. 27). Revelation 17:9 (the seven hills) and 17:18 (the great ruling city) are most naturally understood as alluding to Rome, not Jerusalem.

We should remember that the false prophetess named Jezebel appeared already in 2:20–23. Jezebel represents the same principle that Babylon represents on a worldwide scale. Seduction arises not only outside the church, in the idolatrous culture of the Roman Empire, but also inside the church. People who claim to be Christians try to convince us that compromise with worldly idolatry is really OK. Thus, in our day, seduction comes not only from TV advertisements that promote materialism, but also from false religious teachers. Theological liberalism intends to make peace with the modern world. Health-and-wealth theology claims that we can be rich and healthy, if only we follow the right recipes. The shallow pastor or counselor offers self-help pop psychology rather than the message of sin and redemption as the remedy for our frustrations. Even in apparently orthodox circles, the latest styles of the world are imitated.

The Prostitute rides a hideous beast, evidently the Beast of 13:1–10. The Beast, representing the Roman Empire, supports the city of Rome in its luxurious idolatry. It also spreads the practices of Rome throughout the Empire. Eventually, however, the Beast turns against the Prostitute and destroys her (17:16–17). The rapacious powers of Roman government and the Roman legions would destroy prosperity, and eventually the military powers of the neighboring tribes would destroy the city of Rome itself. The lesson of Roman can be generalized: idolatrous states end up destroying the very powers, riches, privileges, and people that they start out supporting. False worship is self-destructive.

When the destruction of false worship is complete (17:1–18:24), the true worshipers, the bride of the Lamb, stand out in their splendor and joy (19:1–10).

Introducing Babylon (17:1–6)

Even at the beginning of the section on Babylon, the note of punishment and downfall is evident. The angel who appears here is the same one who was involved with the terrible judgments in the preceding cycle, hinting that this section involves further judgment. John sees not simply a vision of Babylon, but of her **punishment** (v. 1). Her punishment is also an indictment of all who are associated with her; they have been corrupted by her corruptions, and hence they will share her fate (v. 2; see 14:8–11). The **many waters** stand for many nations (v. 15), indicating the vast scope of her corrupting influence.

John moves through the Spirit to a new vantage point for the vision (v. 3). Such transports occur elsewhere only at 1:10, 4:1–2, and 21:9–10, underlining the significance of the revelation that will be given.

The Prostitute symbolizes the worldly city (v. 18), including the opulence possible through the power and complexity of cities. Ironically, the scene of her judgment is in **a desert** (v. 3), in austerity. The promises of luxury and pleasure prove in the end to be vain. But at the moment, the woman is impressively luxurious (v. 4).

The woman sits **on a scarlet beast** (v. 3), whose features match the Beast of 13:1–8. In a word, the Prostitute and the Beast cooperate. In the Roman Empire, imperial power (the Beast) undergirded pleasure and wealth (the Prostitute). State power made possible the amassing of wealth. Similarly today, people put their hope in state power, whenever it promises to deliver utopian peace and prosperity. Communist governments have engaged in all kinds of brutality, and yet have received people's allegiance, because totalitarian power was supposedly a necessary means to achieve the utopian communist society.

The woman is dressed in the ostentatious garb of a prostitute (v. 4, cf. Prov. 7:16–17). She combines the lure of sexual pleasure with the lure of luxury. Sensual pleasures of all kinds are available in the city in relative anonymity. But she is deceitful. The long-term consequences are entirely unpleasant. The golden cup looks good on the outside, but it contains **abominable things and the filth of her adulteries** (v. 4). "For the wages of sin is death" (Rom. 6:23; cf. Prov. 7:27). (On the spiritual dimensions of adultery, see 2:20.)

She is called **Babylon** (v. 5), indicating the essential unity of all manifestations of the worldly city. Babel (Gen. 11:1–9), Belshazzar's Babylon (Dan. 5; 7:4; Jer. 50–51), imperial Rome (1 Peter 5:13), the seven cities of Asia (Rev. 1:11), papal Rome, and modern cities can in fact all be rolled together, because the principle is the same. The kingdom of God is opposed by the kingdom of this world (Rev. 11:15, 8). The woman's most heinous crime is her participation in the persecution of the saints (17:6).

The First Angelic Message, Concerning War and the Destruction of Babylon (17:7–18)

As elsewhere in Revelation and other apocalyptic literature, angels explain aspects of mysterious visions (v. 7; cf. 7:13–14; 10:9–11; Dan. 10:10–12:4; Zech. 1:9, 18–21; 2:1–2; 4:4–7). The Beast **once was, now is not, and will come . . .** (v. 8). This description is a counterfeit of the sovereignty of God, which is proclaimed in 1:4, 8; 4:8. "Now is not" indicates that persecution is now at an ebb, but will arise with renewed intensity in the future. The Beast represents a repeated pattern of persecution, as in the four successive beasts of Daniel 7 (see 13:1–10). As in 13:8, the Beast captures the allegiance of all except the elect, whose names have been **written in the book of life.** Their names have been written there **from the creation of the world,** indicating the absolute sovereignty of God and his control over salvation from the beginning (4:11; cf. John 6:37–39). The course of history holds no surprises for God. He knows the end from the beginning, for he is the Alpha and the Omega (1:8; 21:6; 22:13). We are saved not because of superior goodness or intelligence, but through the grace of God, who has undertaken to redeem us from the rest of humanity (14:4). In spiritual warfare, there is no neutral position. Ultimately you are either for God or against him.

Rome was known as the city built on **seven hills.** At the time when John wrote, Rome was the principal embodiment of Babylon, the worldly city. But who are the **seven kings,** five of whom **have fallen?** According to one interpretation, if Revelation was written in about A.D. 67, these five may have been the first five Roman emperors, beginning with Julius Caesar. The sixth would then be Nero, the currently reigning emperor. But in that case, the history of the Empire subsequent to Nero presents us with nothing but problems. After Nero came Galba, Otho, and Vitellius in 68, the "year of three emperors." One may not simply ignore them or skip them in order to arrive at Vespasian (69–79), who ruled at the time of the fall of Jerusalem (70) (see fig. 23). The sixth head is clearly near the end, and is to be succeeded by at most two more manifestations. Hence, this whole line of reasoning must be mistaken. The five who have fallen are simply an indefinite number of previous emperors. The presence of the sixth indicates in symbolic fashion that Christians are near the end, but not quite there. The Beast itself is **an eighth king** (v. 11). Since there are only seven heads, the verse is not claiming that the Beast is an eighth head. Rather, the Beast symbolizes, in its final manifestation, a power analogous to that of the seven.

Fig. 23. The Roman Emperors

• Augustus	27 B.C.–A.D. 14
• Tiberius	A.D. 14–37
• Caligula	37–41
• Claudius	41–54
• **Nero***	54–68
• Galba	68–69
• Otho	69
• Vitellius	69
• **Vespasian***	69–79
• Titus	79–81
• **Domitian***	81–96

*Most plausible options for reigning emperor when Revelation was written.

What then are **the ten horns** (v. 12)? The number ten goes back through 17:7 and 13:1 to Daniel 7:7, 24, where the fourth beast of Daniel 7 has ten horns. But the Beast of Revelation cannot simply be identified with the fourth beast of Daniel. Rather, he is a composite, summing up characteristics of all four of Daniel's beasts. In Revelation, the ten horns are kingly confederates of the Beast. In view of 16:12, 14, 16; 19:19; 20:8, the political powers beyond the borders of the Roman Empire are most directly in mind. Rome was eventually overrun by barbarian tribes. But the picture goes beyond the Roman situation and reaches the final battle in which the Beast will enlist large-scale assistance. The Beast, as an antichrist figure, enlists many other powers who cooperate with him. As archenemies of God, they undertake a final, climactic battle against the Lord and his Anointed (Ps. 2:2; Acts 4:26). The details of the battle unfold in 19:11–21.

Peoples, multitudes, nations and languages (v. 15) reiterates the worldwide scope of the conflict (see on 5:9).

Ironically, God uses evil powers to destroy one another. The Beast and his cohorts turn against the Prostitute (vv. 16–17). Idolatry in all its forms crumbles and falls. Those disappointed with the failure of their idols may turn on the idols and take vengeance. The pattern proved true in the Roman Empire, in that military might, which for a long time upheld the Empire, in the end destroyed it. The same pattern holds for every manifestation of Satan's works throughout this age.

God is ultimately behind the destruction (v. 17). In the midst of trials, the saints are assured that God is in control even of this appalling conflict.

The Second Angelic Message, Announcing Babylon's Fall (18:1–3)

Chapter 18 contains many allusions to Jeremiah 50–51 (prophesying the fall of Babylon) and Ezekiel 27 (prophesying the fall of Tyre).

In Revelation 18:1–3 an angel announces the fall of Babylon (cf. 14:8). Because of his exalted commission, the angel's splendor reflects that of God himself (cf. 10:1; 1:16). As in Jeremiah 50:39, Babylon becomes utterly desolate. Unlike Jerusalem during the Exile, not even a remnant or a shadow of the original city is left. It is not fit for human habitation, but only for wild animals (Isa. 13:20–22). Since the whole picture is symbolic, the usual desert animals of Jeremiah 50:39 and Isaiah 13:20–22 are replaced by **every unclean and detestable bird,** the uncleanness of which stands for the spiritual uncleanness of Babylon. The unclean birds, in turn, symbolize unclean spirits.

All the nations, their kings, and their merchants are implicated, because Babylon has seduced them (cf. 14:8; 17:2). She is not only immoral herself, but has entrapped others, thereby multiplying the guilt (cf. 2:20; Rom. 1:32).

The Third Angelic Message, Warning Saints to Come Out (18:4–8)

A heavenly voice commands the saints to **come out,** that is, to be separate from Babylon's immorality. Purity and spiritual separation from worldliness are a repeated theme in the Bible (see Isa. 48:20; 52:11; Jer. 50:8; 51:6, 45; 2 Cor. 6:17). When the temptations are subtle, as they frequently are in modern societies, vigilance, watchfulness, and understanding of the true nature of spiritual war are necessary. The Bible as a whole summons us to be aware of Satan's schemes (2 Cor. 2:11).

Her sins are piled up to heaven, in an ironic reminiscence of the plan for the tower of Babel to reach to heaven (Gen. 11:4; Jer. 51:9). Fame and power are vain if they are achieved through sinning.

As in 16:5–6, judgment fits the nature of the offense (18:6–7; cf. Ex. 21:23–25). Fire (18:8) is a symbol of God's consuming judgment (see Jer. 50:32; Mal. 4:1; Isa. 66:15–16).

Laments from Friends of Babylon (18:9–20)

Revelation illustrates the wide-ranging scope of Babylon's work and the meaning of her downfall by picturing the reactions of her friends. Kings, merchants, and sailors have been seduced to worship the luxury of Babylon. They have all admired her and profited from her. They are terrified by the destruction that they see, and they stand far off, fearful of getting caught in the destruction (vv. 10, 15, 17). But they do not repent. Instead, they look back longingly to the earlier time of her prosperity, even as Lot's wife looked back longingly at Sodom and Gomorrah.

Cases of hardened wickedness take this very pattern. Even when people know that they are sinning, and when they know that destruction follows, they cannot bear to give up their sins. They cannot give up the pleasures or wealth that they obtain from sin.

The catalog of luxuries in 18:11–13 makes clear how people may indulge themselves at the expense of others ("bodies and souls of men," v. 13). Other people, merchants and sailors, may admire the luxury, but are most interested in the profit that they get from supplying the luxuries to others (vv. 15, 19). In the context of the Roman Empire, the picture was literally true. The powerful ("the kings of the earth") grew rich through the concentration of power in the Roman Empire, and they built their estates on the backs of slaves. Merchants and sailors stood to profit from the trade in luxury items.

Analogous situations are present in modern societies. Those who are in positions of power, whether in government, industry, commerce, or entertainment, grow rich, frequently through unscrupulous practices. Others profit from serving those in power. Typically, such people cannot bear to see a change in the status quo, for it threatens the comfort of their position. But the righteous love righteousness more than any amount of earthly comfort and prosperity.

The powerful weep to see the end of their power to exercise wickedness, but the proper reaction is one of rejoicing (18:20; 19:1–4). Modern societies teach us to love comfort and to abhor all destruction. But this modern attitude is nothing but a false sentimentality. Wickedness needs destruction. It is primarily an offense to God, but also to those who are oppressed by it (18:13).

The Final Announcement of Irrevocable Destruction (18:21–24)

In the seventh and final message of destruction on Babylon, the announcing angel dwells on the completeness and permanence of the destruction. Babylon will never again have any power or resources with which to bring her evils upon the world. The destruction of Babylon is thus a fitting prelude to the vision of a new heaven and a new earth, free from all trouble (21:4).

In a parallel with Jeremiah 51:63–64, the finality of Babylon's fall is depicted by the irreversible act of throwing a large stone into the sea. Then follows a long list announcing the permanent cessation of all kinds of activity (compare Jer. 25:10, predicting the fall of Jerusalem). The heaping up of phrases proclaims like a death knell the certainty of her end. The passage closes, fittingly, with a final reminder of the necessity and justice of her judgment: she was guilty of the blood of martyrs (v. 24).

The Pure Bride, Antithetical to Babylon (19:1–10)

The triumph of the pure bride is contrasted with the destruction of the corrupt, false church (Babylon). Note the repeated hallelujahs (vv. 1, 3, 4, 5, 6). The roar from heaven imitates the thunder of God's own voice. We are probably supposed to think of the entire heavenly company as participating—angelic beings and saints from both Old and New Testament times. The heavenly company rejoices when wickedness is destroyed and righteousness is established (see on 18:20). The judgment is just, fitting Babylon's crimes (see on 15:3).

The description singles out **the twenty-four elders and the four living creatures,** the most prominent angelic servants from 4:4, 6. The focus is on the creatures and their worship, but we must not forget that God is in the center of the picture in Revelation 4. The final celebration of God's victory fittingly takes place in his presence, in the company of the heavenly host (Heb. 12:22–24).

Then **a voice came from the throne** (v. 5), possibly an angelic voice, but in any case a voice expressing God's will. The saints respond in joyful obedience and with heartfelt spontaneity. God's triumph is complete, and that is profoundly satisfying to his saints.

In fact, there is a **wedding** (v. 7). The wedding imagery expresses the intimacy, love, and joy between Christ and his people. It consummates the commitments expressed earlier in Scripture (Hos. 2:19–20; Isa. 54:5–8; Eph. 5:26–27). The wedding feast, the consummation of blessing and satisfaction, contrasts pointedly with the horrific feast of 19:17–18, 21, in which the birds consume the corpses of the wicked. Everyone will participate in one or the other feast.

The fine linen represents **the righteous acts of the saints.** The saints are distinguished from the world by their righteous acts (2 Thess. 1:5; Matt. 25:31–46; 5:16). At the same time, these acts are not the product of autonomous effort, but planned and empowered by God (Eph. 2:10; Phil. 2:12–13).

Revelation 19:9 underlines the trustworthiness and certainty of God's word, as the book does elsewhere (21:5; 22:6; cf. 1:2, 5). The angel bears a divine message and reflects God's splendor. John is overwhelmed with the weight of it all, and in confusion starts to worship the mediating angel (v. 10; cf. 22:9). The angel therefore reminds him that the angels also are servants, alongside Christians (cf. Heb. 1:14).

The Appearing of Christ and the Final Battle (19:11–21)

In 19:11–21 Christ appears as the divine warrior to wage war against all the enemies of God, led by the Beast and the False Prophet. Christ's holy attributes contrast markedly with the unholy attributes of the Beast (13:1–10). This final battle brings to a climax all the wars that God has waged on behalf of his people (Ex. 15:2; Deut. 20; Hab. 3:8–15; Isa. 59:16–18; Ezek. 38–39; Zech. 12:1–9; 14:3–5) and consummates the triumph achieved by Christ on the cross (John 12:31; Col. 2:15; Rev. 5:9–10; 12:10–11).

Some have interpreted this imagery as a reference to the spread of Christ's rule through conversion to Christianity. But the parallels with 16:14, 16, 17:14, and 20:7–10 show that the final battle is primarily in view (see on 16:14 and 16:17–21). The section 19:11–21 constitutes the sixth cycle of judgments leading to the Second Coming (see "Structure" in the Introduction). In the later cycles, the imagery concentrates more and more intensively on the Second Coming and its immediate precursors. In this cycle, all the events are actually part of the Second Coming. But, as is typical of Revelation, they bring into full manifestation principles of spiritual warfare that have been operative throughout the church age (1 John 5:4–5; Eph. 6:10–20). At the end, Jesus Christ is revealed fully as who he always is (Rev. 22:13; Heb. 13:8).

The Appearing of Christ (19:11–16)

Heaven stands **open.** God reveals his presence not merely to John, as in 4:1, but to the whole world of humanity. The appearance of the divine warrior in his majesty must mean the end of the battle and the destruction of all enemies before him.

Christ bears worthy names (vv. 11–12, 16), in contrast to the blasphemous names on the Beast (13:1). During this age, he has been the faithful and true witness (1:5), identifying with the suffering and martyrdom of his saints that witness on earth (cf. 11:7). At his coming, he appears as the faithful and true warrior and *judge* (cf. Isa. 11:4). The wars of earthly armies typically leave much unjust suffering and destruction in their wake. This war, however, is utterly just, because of the supreme power and justice of the One who wages war.

Other aspects of the vision also testify to his worthiness and authority for the task. The **eyes like blazing fire,** recalling 1:14 and 2:18, affirm Christ's ability to see and judge human hearts and not merely outward appearance (2:23; Isa. 11:3–5; 1 Sam. 16:7). The **many crowns** on his head indicate the legitimate kingly authority that he has from the Father. The **name that no one knows** (v. 12) indicates that the full and surprising aspects of his coming are still a mystery to all. It may also remind us of his transcendence, his deity (cf. Judg. 13:18, 22). The name **Word of God,** as in John 1:1, reminds us of his powerful role in creation (Gen. 1:3; Ps. 33:6) and providence (Ps. 147:15; Lam. 3:37–38; Heb. 1:3). By virtue of his divinity and his lordship over all, he has the ability to bring to a conclusion the history that he has ruled over from the beginning (Isa. 11:4).

The significance of the **robe dipped in blood** is ambiguous. Some think that Christ's own blood, the blood that redeems the saints, is in view (5:9). This view is possible, because Christ's sacrifice is the key to the working out of God's plan for all of history, including its consummation (5:2–6). But the picture developed in 19:13 has close affinities with Isaiah 63:2–3, where God as the divine warrior spatters his garment with the blood of his enemies whom he tramples in the winepress (as in Rev. 19:15). The context in Revelation 19 is one where Christ destroys his enemies in blood, not one where he redeems the saints. Hence, the connection with Isaiah 63:2–3 is the significant one.

The armies of heaven (v. 14) imitate their leader. They too ride on white horses, and they have his purity. In the Old Testament, the heavenly armies consist of angels. Possibly the saints are included at this point, but there is no explicit indication of that (but note 17:14). In any case, these armies have no distinct role in the battle. The achievement and the glory belong to Christ, and all the focus is appropriately on him. His weapon is the sharp sword, as in 1:16, representing his all-powerful word (see Eph. 6:17; Isa. 11:4; Heb. 4:12).

Christ rules the nations **with an iron scepter,** in fulfillment of Psalm 2:9, where his rule is further described as dashing the nations to pieces. He destroys the nations in rebellion (Rev. 19:19–21). The Bible as a whole, as well as Revelation, indicates that the Second Coming is for the purpose of salvation and renewal of the world (21:1–8), as well as destruction. But 19:11–21 focuses on the destructive aspects. Evil must be destroyed, not only for the sake of God's justice, but for the sake of the purity of the new world (21:27).

The Battle (19:17–21)

Now an angelic messenger stands **in the sun.** He reflects the brightness of God's glory and calls to mind the great theophanies of chapter 4 and other passages in the Bible. This reflection of God's splendor is also a reminder that his message has God's authority and expresses his plan.

The angel summons birds to a horrific supper. Building on the imagery of Ezekiel 39:4, 17–20, it depicts God's curse on rebels. The curse includes not only death for the wicked, but the dishonoring of their bodies after death. Instead of receiving honorable burial, their bodies are devoured by birds (cf. Gen. 40:19; Deut. 28:26; 1 Sam. 17:44; 2 Sam. 21:10; 1 Kings 14:11). It is the opposite of the blessed supper of the Lamb in 19:9. (On the Beast and the False Prophet, see 13:1–18.) The gathering armies fill out the picture already introduced in 16:14.

The fiery lake of burning sulfur (v. 20) is hell, the final abode of the wicked (20:10, 14–15; 21:8; 14:10–11; cf. Isa. 66:24). Fire is frequently associated with all-consuming judgment (cf. Joel 2:3; Isa. 66:15–16).

The Judgments (20:1–21:8)

The seventh cycle of judgment includes the one-thousand-year reign of the saints (20:1–10) and the last judgment in its negative (20:11–15) and positive aspects (21:1–8).

This final cycle wraps up the course of history by dealing with several issues of justice. God vindicates the saints, giving an answer for their past suffering and martyrdom (20:4–6). He executes final judgment on Satan, the source of evil, thus eliminating the last of the three evil scourges in the world. (The Prostitute was eliminated in 17:1–19:10, and the Beast and the False Prophet were eliminated in 19:11–21.) He pronounces comprehensive judgment; nothing escapes his attention (20:11–15). He creates a new world free from the evils, sufferings, and rebellion of the old world (21:1–8).

The One-Thousand-Year Reign (20:1–10)

The one-thousand-year reign promises relief to persecuted saints.

An angel descending from heaven binds Satan for a thousand years. The faithful martyrs (20:4) come to life and reign with Christ. After the thousand years, Satan is released, gathers the nations for battle, and is finally rendered powerless (20:10).

Biblical interpreters have differed in their interpretation of the one-thousand-year period, commonly called the Millennium. *Premillennialists* believe that the one thousand years follow the Second Coming, which has just been described in 19:11–21.

177

After the Second Coming, in their view, Satan is bound and Christ ushers in a long period of earthly peace and prosperity—some think of a literal one thousand years, while others consider the number to be simply a symbol for a very long period of time. Christians receive resurrection bodies at the beginning of the Millennium, but the final judgment for all others takes place at the end of it, after a rebellion led by Satan. In the second century, Papias and Justin Martyr were among those holding a premillennial view.

Amillennialists understand the Millennium to be a picture of the present reign of Christ and of the saints in heaven (analogous to 6:9–10). The first resurrection, on this view, is either the life of disembodied Christians with Christ in heaven (6:9–10) or life in Christ that starts with the new birth (Rom. 6:8–11; Col. 3:1–4; Eph. 2:6). Satan has been bound through the triumph of Christ in his crucifixion and resurrection (John 12:31; Col. 2:15).

Postmillennialists believe that the kingdom of Christ and the church will experience much more expansion on earth before the Second Coming. Some postmillennialists understand the one thousand years as a final period of Christian earthly triumph following the spread of the gospel in 19:11–21. Other postmillennialists agree with amillennialists in identifying 20:1–6 with the entire period beginning with the resurrection of Christ.

Caution is needed because the different millennial positions depend on the interpretation of Old Testament prophetic texts as well as 20:1–10. Moreover, like most of Revelation, 20:1–10 uses language that in principle may have more than one concrete embodiment. These facts make precise interpretation more difficult. The major point is that Satan will be finally defeated, and that even before that time God takes care of his saints and gives them enjoyment of the benefits of his triumphant rule. This assurance ought to comfort us, whatever our millennial position.

The millennial dispute partly has to do with the chronological relationship between 19:11–21 and 20:1–10 . Premillennialists

believe that the events of 20:1–10 simply follow the events depicted in 19:11–21, which places the Millennium after the
Second Coming. However, in view of the structure of the whole
book, it makes more sense to see 20:1–15 as the seventh and last
cycle of judgments, each of which leads up to the Second
Coming. Several pieces of evidence point in this direction:

- The final battle in 20:7–10 seems to be the same as the final battle in 16:14, 16; 17:14; 19:11–21.
- The various descriptions of the final battle use language
  that is similar to that in Ezekiel 38–39.
- The judgment of Satan in 20:10 parallels the judgments of
  Babylon (chapters 17–18) and of the Beast and the False
  Prophet (19:11–21). These enemies of God all receive their
  doom, and the visions depicting their doom are thematically rather than chronologically arranged.
- Certain features in 20:11–15 correspond to earlier descriptions of the Second Coming (6:14; 11:18).
- Most importantly, all of Christ's enemies are destroyed in
  19:11–21. If 20:1–6 describes events later than 19:11–21,
  there would be no one left for Satan to deceive in 20:3.

Thus, 20:1–15 is to be seen as the seventh cycle leading to the
Second Coming. It parallels all the other cycles, rather than representing a unique period chronologically later than any of the
others (see "Structure" in the Introduction).

The mention of **the first resurrection** in 20:5–6 is often
seen as evidence in favor of premillennialism. It is argued that
resurrections are by definition bodily, and so "the first resurrection" must be a bodily resurrection. And since no one is resur-
rected until the Second Coming, all the events of 20:1–10 must
be subsequent to it.

However, the situation is more complex than that. The expression "first resurrection" obviously implies that there is a second one. Similarly, the mention of **the second death** in 20:6

clearly implies that there is a first death. In this context, the first and second resurrections would seem to be related to the first and second deaths. And we know from the general teaching of Scripture what both of these deaths are. The first death is bodily death (1 Cor. 15:22; Heb. 9:27). The second death is consignment to hell, the final abode of the wicked (Rev. 20:14–15). The second death is *spiritual* in character, and accompanies bodily resurrection (John 5:28–29). The first death is preliminary, while the second death is final and irreversible. As there are a first heaven and earth and a second or last heaven and earth (Rev. 21:1), so there are a first death and a last death. Moreover, the first death, as a curse, is a sign of the coming of the more terrible second death (cf. Gen. 3:19).

These facts provide the decisive clues for understanding the first and second resurrections. The first resurrection, like the first death, is preliminary, while the second resurrection, like the second death, is final. The second resurrection is clearly bodily resurrection. It is clearly the remedy for the first death, bodily death. Conversely, the first resurrection is a kind of remedy for the second death, according to Revelation 20:6. That is, the first resurrection guarantees freedom from the second death. The various symmetries suggest that the first resurrection, like the second death, is paradoxical in character. As the second death implicitly includes and accompanies an act of bodily resurrection, so the first resurrection implicitly includes and accompanies bodily death. We find an allusion to this bodily death in 20:4, **the souls of those who had been beheaded.** This phrase refers to those who have suffered martyrdom for not worshiping the Beast. These are now disembodied souls, living in the presence of God and of Christ, as represented in 6:9–10. The important thing to see is that these souls are *living,* triumphant, because of their union with Christ and their victory through his blood (12:11). The assertion and enjoyment of their triumph is not simply postponed until the Second Coming. They enjoy victory even at the moment of death, for God places them in positions of authority and judgment in the heavenly realms (on **thrones,** v. 4). The earthly authorities who condemned them to death are already beaten by this greater authority that the saints exercise in heaven.[22]

The picture in 20:4–6 thus answers a pressing question during times of intense persecution. When Christians are a weak minority, when great imperial powers are arrayed against them, is there any hope for victory? What happens when Christians are viciously put to death? It appears to the world that they have been decisively defeated. The persecuting authorities are very much alive and as powerful as ever, while Christians have been simply wiped out. Christianity appears to be a hopelessly weak religion. Does God not care? Is he really in control? Can anything undo the defeat that Christians have suffered through their martyrdom? Revelation 20:4–6 answers that heavenly realities must be included in assessing the situation. And when we see these realities, the tables are completed turned. It turns out that it is impossible to defeat Christians. Even when demonic forces are ravaging the church, they are only establishing Christians in positions of real and permanent power!

Now let us consider some of the details. Satan is **bound,** meaning that his power to influence the nations is suppressed. Premillennialists and some postmillennialists associate this event with the advent of an extraordinary era of peace and prosperity in the future—unlike the present, when Satan is powerful (1 Thess. 2:18; 1 Peter 5:8). But on the amillennial interpretation, Satan has already been bound through Christ's death and resurrection (John 12:31; cf. Col. 2:15; Rev. 12:9; Matt. 12:29). The present spread of the gospel to the nations, as initiated in Acts, is the result of a major restriction on Satan's power to deceive. Possibly this restriction on Satan's power is associated with the present temporary demise of the Beast (Rev. 17:8). The deceiving of the nations takes place largely through the activity of the Beast (13:14; 16:14; 19:20). As the Beast can suffer repeated defeats (17:8, 10), so Satan can suffer repeated reverses in his power over the nations. The loosing of Satan in 20:7–10 would then represent his final attempt to deceive the nations, leading to his final defeat.

Who are **the souls** (v. 4)? As in 6:9–10, martyrs are singled out as the most notable group of faithful witnesses. But other saints are not excluded from the privileges mentioned. The reigning of the saints in verse 4 is promised in 2:26–27 and 3:21.

What is **the first resurrection?** If this resurrection is a bodily resurrection, it coincides with the Second Coming (1 Cor. 15:51–57; 1 Thess. 4:13–18). Then the premillennialists are right (see above). But the correlations between the first and second deaths and the first and second resurrections suggest that the first resurrection refers to the spiritual life of martyrs who reign with Christ between the time of their martyrdom and the Second Coming.

Gog and Magog (v. 8) are names from Ezekiel 38–39 that represent the final enemies of God. Having been loosed, Satan is finally able to gather the nations to battle, as in 16:14. His desire all through history has been to muster the human race into united opposition to God, and now he finally achieves his desire, after a fashion. But opposing God is always futile. Satan summons the nations only to experience his final doom.

The Judgment (20:11–15)

In 20:11–15 God appears in a scene of final judgment. His authority to judge has already been anticipated in chapters 4 and 5. Now he executes the judgment that befits his character and power over the created universe, as was earlier displayed in 4:1–11. The vision in 20:11–15 shares features with Matthew 25:31–46 and such Old Testament judgment scenes as Daniel 7:9–10 and Psalms 7:6–8; 47:8–9.

Injustice and suffering never escape God's eye. Those who persecute and those who practice injustice can never win. God will judge every deed, all wrongs will be righted, and all attempts to dethrone God and enthrone oneself will be completely frustrated. The prospect of final judgment ought to be a terror to God's enemies and a foundation of assurance to the saints.

This judgment follows the one thousand years of 20:2, 7. Premillennialists believe that the Second Coming precedes the one thousand years, and hence must include a distinct judgment of its own. In their view, Christians receive their reward at the Second Coming, and this later judgment is for the wicked and those living in untransformed bodies during the one thousand years. Amillennialists and postmillennialists, on the other hand, have generally understood this passage as one of many references to a universal final judgment at the Second Coming (see on 20:1–10).

The **throne** of God symbolizes his power, his authority, and his ability to exercise righteous and thorough judgment (see 4:2).

The **sky fled,** as in 6:14. The **book of life,** the roster of God's elect people, symbolizes that he knows his own sheep (John 10:3, 27), keeps them all, and loses none of them (John 6:39; 10:28–29; cf. Rev. 13:8). **The lake of fire,** or hell, demonstrates God's consummate justice and his utter frustration of all the devices of wickedness. The new heaven and the new earth will be free from all that has contaminated the world in the first order of things.

The New Heaven and the New Earth (21:1–8)

The section 21:1–8, concerning the new heaven and the new earth, is usually grouped together with 21:9–22:5. The two passages present two aspects of the final vision of the new Jerusalem. Many of the features that are introduced in 21:1–8 appear with greater elaboration in 21:9–22:5. The first section consists primarily of announcements of the new realities, while the second one contains more visionary description of those realities. But 21:1–8 is also closely related to 20:11–15. The final judgment of God in fact has two sides: the negative side, the judgment of the wicked, is described in 20:11–15, while the positive side, the reward for the righteousness, is described in

21:1–8. Within the negative message of 20:11–15, one finds a positive message in the mention of the book of life at the end (v. 15). Similarly, within the positive message of 21:1–8, one finds a negative message in the mention of the fiery lake at the end (v. 8). Thus, 20:11–15 and 21:1–8 symmetrically depict the negative and positive sides of God's judgment. We see, then, that 21:1–8 is a bridge between the judgment of 20:11–15 and the extended description of the new Jerusalem in 21:9–22:5.

The voice of God announces the descent of the new Jerusalem against the backdrop of total renovation: a new heaven and a new earth. God is the Alpha (see 1:8), the Creator, whose purposes have been expressed from the beginning. Now he shows himself to be the Omega, the Consummator, who brings his purposes to final realization. The vision of his throne in 4:1–11 displayed his glory, power, and beauty within the sphere of heaven. But now the dwelling of God is with all his people (21:3). All the pain and suffering that run through the earlier parts of Revelation are now abolished. All the promises made to those who overcome are now fulfilled (see 2:7).

This vision is meant to encourage faithfulness, confidence, and hope in Christians, especially those who face persecution. God will fully achieve his purpose, and Christians will inherit his full blessing, however grim the present circumstances may be. Although this vision pertains to the consummation of all things, in Christ we even now receive a foretaste of our future inheritance (Eph. 1:14; Heb. 12:18–29). God's promises should stimulate our fervent devotion to Christ.

The final visions of Revelation weave into a beautiful unity a host of themes from the rest of the Bible. Notice the themes of creation (v. 1), the holy city of Jerusalem (v. 2), communion with God expressed through marriage imagery (v. 2), the dwelling of God, including the tabernacle and the temple (v. 3; see on 4:1–5:14), the saints as God's own people (v. 3), the end of suffering and death (v. 4), new saving acts (v. 5), the trustworthiness of God's word (v. 5), living water (v. 6), becoming a son of God (v. 7), warnings to the faithless (v. 8), and judgment (v. 8).

God creates **a new heaven and a new earth,** which implies comprehensive renovation. Some have thought that the new universe will be an entirely new one, having no connection with the old. But Isaiah 65:17–25 and Romans 8:21–23 indicate that a transfiguration of the old world is in view, like the way in which our new bodies will be transfigurations of our old ones (1 Cor. 15:35–57). Everything is new (21:5), but the result is the redemption of the old, not its abolition. Some people are prone to worry about the loss of things from this life. Indeed, we must be prepared to give up everything for the sake of loyalty to Christ (Luke 9:23–26; 14:25–35; John 12:24–26). But in the process we will find that nothing of genuine value is permanently lost. After all, God in his beauty and majesty is the source for all beauty and joy that we have as creatures, and we will get to live in the presence of God himself (Rev. 21:3; 22:4–5). We do not know the details of what God will do and how he will do it. But we do know that his presence means consummate joy (19:9). We will have no regrets or unsatisfiable longings (21:4).

Why is there **no longer any sea?** The description here is symbolic. We will not lose the beauty and awe that modern people associate with the sea and its creatures. Rather, we will lose evil and chaos that ancient people associated with the sea. Water destroyed the world at the time of Noah. Overwhelming waters picture the coming of death (Pss. 42:7; 69:1; Jonah 2:3). From the sea rise terrible monsters (Dan. 7:3; Isa. 27:1; 51:9–10; Rev. 13:1). The removal of the sea means the permanent removal of all challenges to God's order, and hence the peace and stability of the new world.

At the center of the new creation is the new holy city, representing the dwelling of God with his people. In the Old Testament, Jerusalem was the place where the Lord God put his name and where he established his dwelling place (Deut. 12:5, 11; 1 Kings 8:16, 29). God establishes a place where not only individuals, but the whole nation, can have access to him, can obtain forgiveness, and can bring their prayers and their offerings. The temple and the surrounding city are consecrated for the presence of God, to be the way of access to him. In Christ, this access to God is fulfilled. He is the "one mediator between God and men" (1 Tim. 2:5). The whole international community of saints has access even now to the heavenly assembly (Heb. 12:18–29). The new Jerusalem represents the perfecting of the community and the consummation of its joy in the presence of God. This consummation is fundamentally the work of God, not of human beings. It is not Babel reaching up to assault heaven in autonomous pride, but the new Jerusalem **coming down out of heaven** as the gift and artistic product of God's craft.

The imagery shifts from the city to the bride (v. 2), further personalizing the picture and stressing the intimacy, love, and pleasure of communion with God (cf. 19:7–9; Eph. 5:22–33; Song of Solomon).

God dwelt with human beings in the Garden of Eden (Gen. 2:7, 16; 3:8), in the tabernacle (Ex. 25:8; 40:34), in the temple (1 Kings 8), and above all in Christ (John 1:14; 2:19–21). Christ sends forth the Spirit in order that the church (1 Cor. 3:16) and its members (1 Cor. 6:19) may be dwellings of God. The new Jerusalem is the consummation of all of these. God will be **their God,** implying that he will be a faithful and loving supplier of all their needs, with unimaginable fullness. All the commitments and promises of God throughout history find the apex of their fulfillment. Positively, there is consummate blessing; negatively, all aspects of suffering and frustration are completely removed (v. 4). God himself guarantees the certainty and the effectiveness of this result (v. 5), on the basis of his own sovereignty and competence as Creator (v. 6). Full satisfaction is represented by the water of life (v. 6). Many passages associate living water first of all with the Holy Spirit, and then subordinately with the blessings that the Holy Spirit brings (Rev. 22:1; 7:17; John 4:10; 7:37–38; Isa. 44:3; 55:1; Zech. 14:8; Joel 3:18; Ezek. 47).

Both as a warning and as a guarantee, verse 8 notes that the wicked will be excluded from the new Jerusalem. This exclusion summarizes the point already made in 20:11–15. The standard of God's justice, as well as the holiness and the peace of the new Jerusalem, requires the exclusion of evil. No sin or second fall into evil will disturb the permanent security and bliss of the new world.

The New Jerusalem (21:9–22:5)

The picture of the new Jerusalem is now unfolded in detail. The final dwelling place of the saints is simultaneously the fulfillment of earlier revelations of (1) God appearing in glory and reigning in his heavenly court (compare 22:1, 3 and 21:22–23 with 4:1–11), (2) the holy city of Jerusalem (21:10), (3) the Garden of Eden (22:1–3), (4) the bride, the marriage partner of the Lord (21:9), and (5) the temple as God's dwelling place (21:3, 22). At the center of the city is God himself and the Lamb (21:22–23; 22:1–5). The final revelation of God necessarily brings to a climax all earlier revelations. It completes God's purpose of bringing all things under one head, even Christ (11:15; Eph. 1:10). This harmonizes with the creation of all things by Christ at the beginning (Rev. 4:11; 1:17; Col. 1:15–17) and the redemption of all things through Christ in the middle (Rev. 5:9–14; Col. 1:18–20; Rom. 11:36). Because of the fluid character of the imagery, it is wisest not to distinguish rigidly between the inhabitants of the city (the saints) and the city itself (the saints together with the glorified creation).

The Architecture of the New Jerusalem (21:9–27)

As in 21:2, the new city is called the bride (v. 9). As a bride, we enjoy personal intimacy and joy in the presence of God; as a city, we enjoy structural organization with other saints in a harmonious worldwide community.

The mention of being **in the Spirit** reiterates 1:10; 4:1; 17:3. The Spirit transports John to a new vantage point for this final vision, underlining its importance. The mountain location reminds us of God's special meeting place with people, alluding to 14:1 (see also Ex. 15:17; 19:1–25; Pss. 48:1–2; 68:15–16; Ezek. 28:14; Mic. 4:1–2).

The fundamental character of the city is that it shines with **the glory of God** (v. 11). Being closely associated with the imagery of light, glory indicates the majesty, awesomeness, and beauty of God. Glory is a prominent theme in 21:9–22:5. It is associated with the temple and the appearing of God in the Old Testament (Rev. 21:22–23; 22:5; 15:8; Ex. 16:10; 24:16–17; 40:34–35; Isa. 6:3; 40:5; 60:1–2, 19–20; Hab. 2:14; Zech. 2:5; John 1:14). God's heavenly splendor, as seen in 4:1–11, now fills the new world.

In ancient cities, gates and walls served for protection. Because of the abolition of all evil (21:4, 8), the city has no need of protection in a literal sense. But the imagery remains, to remind us of the full security and architectural wisdom of the whole (cf. Ezek. 40).

The number twelve also has symbolic significance. The twelve tribes of Israel formed the holy people of God in the Old Testament. The church under the teaching and leadership of the twelve apostles forms the holy people of God in the New Testament. The integrity and careful organization of the people is stressed by the use of the number twelve. The foundation is the twelve apostles, because in their teaching and leading functions they point us to Christ (Eph. 2:20; 3:5; 4:11; 1 Cor. 12:28; 3:11!).

The process of measurement, as in Ezekiel 40–41 and Revelation 11:1–2, symbolizes the commitment to preserve the whole, not only in memory, but in actual structural integrity. The dimensions of the city have symbolic significance. Each side is 12,000 stadia. The number twelve symbolizes the people of God, of which this city is the dwelling place. The number one thousand multiplies the dimensions so that the city is absolutely huge: about 1,400 miles on each side. This huge size symbolizes the immensity and profundity of God's purposes that will be realized. There is no lack of space or lack of supplies for the new world. Note also that the city is in the shape of a perfect cube: all three dimensions are the same. The shape is the same as the Most Holy Place in the tabernacle and the temple, but now immensely magnified. Thus, the whole city is not only architecturally perfect, but has become the most intimate dwelling place of God (21:22–23; 22:4).

The wall is **144 cubits** thick (21:17). The number 144 is twelve squared. All the dimensions of the city symbolize its associations with the twelve tribes of Israel and the twelve apostles (21:12, 14). The number twelve symbolically designates the people of God.

There now follows a list of jewels and precious things, expressing the overwhelming riches, beauty, and splendor of the whole city. It has become in its whole and in every part a reflection of the riches, beauty, and splendor of God, as earlier revealed in chapter 4. The list of jewels corresponds roughly to the twelve precious stones of Aaron's breastpiece (Ex. 28:15–21). The prerogatives that once belonged exclusively to the high priest are now reflected in the entire city.

There is no temple, because God is present in his full immediacy in the whole city (see on 4:1–5:14). Previously, **the sun** and **the moon** represented the splendor of God in the heavens, but they are made superfluous by the brightness supplied directly by God. The magnified brightness of the light fulfills Isaiah 60:19–20.

The nations (Rev. 21:24) represent redeemed humanity in all its cultural divisions. The distinctiveness of different cultures and peoples is not simply wiped out, but redeemed, in harmony with the picture in 1 Corinthians 12 of the unity and diversity in the body of Christ (see Isa. 60:3–12; Rev. 5:9). The nations bring in **their splendor,** that is, all the diversity of riches, whether material, intellectual, artistic, or spiritual (Isa. 60:3–5; Hag. 2:7–9).

Ancient city gates needed to be shut in case of attack. But the gates of new Jerusalem need never be shut, in fulfillment of Isaiah 60:11.

As in Revelation 20:11–15 and 21:8, all uncleanness and corruption is excluded (21:27). (On the book of life in v. 27, see 13:8).

The New Jerusalem as the New Garden of Eden (22:1–5)

The final description of the new Jerusalem contains many elements that allude to the Garden of Eden. The intimacy of God with his people (22:3–4) and the abundance of his blessing (22:1–2, 5) are stressed even more than in the preceding passage. The final state restores the unbroken, idyllic communion between God and man. But the apex of history is ever so much more magnificent than the beginning. The garden is now also a city, and the light has completely driven out the night.

Revelation is designed not only to assure us of God's final purposes, but also to increase our longing for him and the realization of his purpose. The sureness of that final bliss comforts the saints during times of temptation and persecution. It purifies our desires by directing them to God and his glory. And then the tawdry counterfeits of this world are seen to be what they are. We have eyes to see the beauties and joys of this creation as pointers to God and his goodness (Acts 14:17), rather than foolishly perverting created things into idols (Rom. 1:18–23).

The center of the new world is God himself and the Lamb. Their rule and control, symbolized by the throne, produce the beauty and blessing of the new world. An abundant supply of life-giving water comes from God. In the picture of the river, Revelation weaves together allusions to Genesis 2:10–14, Psalm 46:4, Ezekiel 47:1–12, Joel 3:18, and John 4:10–14; 7:37–39. The brightness of the river (**clear as crystal**) reflects the glory of God (21:11, 23). The tree of life is present, renewing the blessing of Eden in Genesis 2:9. Access to God's life-giving blessings, barred after the Fall, is here renewed (Gen. 3:22–24; Ezek. 47:12; Rev. 2:7; 22:14, 19). It is not clear how many trees are there (cf. Ezek. 47:12), but in the symbolic mode of Revelation, this detail is not important. The point is that Eden is back, with its fullness of blessing multiplied many times.

The leaves are **for the healing of the nations** (v. 2). The new world has already been described as free from all problems and suffering (21:4). So how can the nations need healing? Actually, we should not read the passage so unimaginatively as to infer that literal sickness is present. A visionary passage like this one weaves together symbolic themes without lending itself to mechanical logic. This language reflects Ezekiel 47:12, but extends the healing not just to Israel but to all nations, in fulfillment of the promise made to Abraham (Gen. 12:3). The new creation as a whole answers all our needs and produces a consummate remedy for all the ills that belonged to the old (21:4).

The theme of returning to Eden continues with the reversal of the curse (v. 3), which answers Genesis 3:14–19. God now exercises his rule entirely by giving blessings. At the heart of this blessing is communion with God himself: seeing his face (v. 4). Our knowledge of God can never exhaust the infinity of his being. But this final knowledge brings the apex of intimacy and enjoyment. At that point, we experience perfect holiness and freedom from sin, and so we can enjoy a vision of God that was not possible while we were contaminated with sin (Ex. 19:21; 33:20; Judg. 13:22; Isa. 6:5; John 1:18).

Light is a symbol of ethical purity, and is closely associated with God (1 John 1:5–7; 2:8–11; John 1:4; 3:19–21). It is fitting, therefore, that the final vision is characterized by pervasive light, without darkness (Rev. 22:5). All evil is gone, and the splendor of God's presence fills the universe.

Closing Exhortations (22:6–21)

The central, visionary part of Revelation ends with 22:5. Revelation now concludes with promise, exhortation, and confirmation, in order to drive home to our hearts the message of the visions, and to stir up hope for the coming of the Lord Jesus (22:20). The major themes of Revelation continue to be woven into this concluding section. There are many allusions back to chapter 1.

The words of Revelation are **trustworthy and true,** echoing 1:2. The theme of witness runs through the entirety of Revelation. Christ is the preeminent witness (1:5), John communicates this witness through the book of Revelation (1:2–3), and the saints take up the task of witness in the face of opposition (2:10, 13; 11:3–12).

Jesus promises to come **soon** (22:7). As in 1:1, the shortness of the time is from the standpoint of Old Testament prophecy, especially Daniel. Daniel prophesied about things that were distant in time. John prophesies about things that are even now in the process of realization, since the resurrection and ascension of Jesus Christ. Saints are always supposed to be watchful, not knowing when the Lord will come (Mark 13:32–37; Luke 12:35–48; 17:20–37). Blessed are those who are awake and watchful, and blessed likewise are the people who take to heart the prophecy of Revelation, which calls us to this same watchfulness and faithfulness to the Master.

The temptation to worship the assisting angel repeats 19:10.

The instruction not to seal up the book (v. 10) underlines the nearness of fulfillment. By contrast with Revelation, Daniel's scroll was sealed because the time of fulfillment was distant (Dan. 12:4).

Verse 11 exhorts us to perseverance in doing right. Under persecution, oppression, and discouragement, saints are tempted to lose heart and compromise. The call to persevere in the faith is always apt (cf. Heb. 10:35–39; 3:6). But how do we understand the pronouncements about continuing to do wrong? The working out of history polarizes good and evil. If people do not repent when they hear the word of God, it increases their hardness. If hearing Revelation does not change one's course of life, it fixes one more firmly to one's present course, on whichever side of the battle that may be (see Dan. 12:10; Ezek. 3:27; 2 Cor. 2:15–16).

On the promise of coming **soon,** see 1:1 and 22:7. God distributes rewards and punishments according to what people have done, as in 20:12. The saints are saved by the grace of God in the work of Christ (19:8; 5:9–10; 13:8; cf. Eph. 2:1–10). But they are not saved in order to continue in sin (Rev. 2:4; 3:3–4; 14:4–5). Even during this life, the saints begin to live a holy life, and God is pleased to reward them for their works (Rev. 2:7, 11, 17, 23–26; 3:3–5, 12, 21; 19:8). The imperfections in these works, and the remaining contaminations from sinful inclinations, are covered by the blood of Christ. Good works are not the basis for eternal life, as if we earned life through our own efforts, but they are demonstrations of the genuineness of our faith and of the justice of God's judgment (1 Peter 1:7; 2 Thess. 1:5). The separation between the righteous and the wicked in 22:14–15 distinguishes people with two antithetical kinds of character and behavior (cf. Matt. 25:31–46). (On the Alpha and the Omega in verse 13, see 1:8.)

The time of consummation has not yet come. But it will come. By picturing the final triumph of God and the splendors to follow, Revelation stirs up our longing for that final day. **The**

Spirit leads the church in prayer: **"Come!"** (22:17). That is, **Come, Lord Jesus** (v. 20). **The bride,** that is, the church (19:7; Eph. 5:22–33), takes up the prayer and longing, as she is taught by the Spirit (cf. Rom. 8:15–16). Revelation continues with an address to the thirsty: "Whoever is thirsty, let him come" (v. 17). Because of this, some interpreters have seen all the occurrences of "come" as addressed to thirsty human beings. But the atmosphere of anticipating the Second Coming makes it more probable that the first two occurrences are addressed to Christ, in longing for his coming. The invitation to the thirsty is then a surprise twist. But it harmonizes with the urgency of the nearness of the Second Coming, as this nearness is underlined by the first two occurrences of "come." The door is open for repentance. The invitation extends both to those who already trust in Christ and to those who are still in rebellion. Come while there is still time, before the Lord comes.

Revelation 22:18–19 reminds us that God's word is holy; it is distinguished from all merely human words. No person is authorized to add to or subtract from the word of God (Deut. 4:2; 12:32; Prov. 30:6; cf. Eccl. 3:14). Revelation underlines its character as the word of God by explicitly prohibiting tampering. God's word is sure, and needs no "updating" or supposed "improvements." Jezebel and the false teachers mentioned in 2:14–15, 20 claimed to be Christians, but they distorted the truth. Such tampering remains a real possibility throughout church history. It may take the form of claims to special visions, as is shown by such later false writings as the Apocalypse of Peter, the Apocalypse of Paul, and the Apocalypse of Thomas. Claims of supposed visions and angelic revelations have continued to be made down to the present day (for example, by Emanuel Swedenborg and Joseph Smith). In addition, teachers who do not claim to have special visions may distort the truth. Like Jezebel, they may try to convince Christians that they can compromise with the ways of the world in order to avoid persecution.[23] (On **the tree of life,** see 22:2.)

Come, Lord Jesus. The whole book of Revelation is meant to stir our longings and prayers for the full realization of God's purposes, which will take place at the Second Coming. Revelation fittingly ends on this note (see 1 Cor. 16:22). Come, Lord Jesus!

Endnotes

1. In the original context, v. 3 refers to people who read Revelation aloud in a church meeting. The reading and hearing of the Bible in church remains important today and needs greater attention than it usually receives. But the point applies indirectly to those who read and hear in other situations.

2. Tremper Longman III, "The Divine Warrior: The New Testament Use of an Old Testament Motif," *Westminster Theological Journal* 44 (1982): 290–307.

3. Ray Summers, *Worthy Is the Lamb* (Nashville: Broadman, 1951), 158.

4. E. B. Elliott, *Horae Apocalypticae* (London: Seeley, Jackson, and Halliday, 1862), 1:435.

5. Ibid., 438.

6. Ibid., 463.

7. "They are extraordinary and infernal agents, whom Satan is permitted to let loose upon the guilty world, as a part of the judgment of the great day." J. A. Seiss, *The Apocalypse* (New York: Cook, 1900), 2:92.

8. William Hendriksen, *More Than Conquerors* (Grand Rapids: Baker, 1961), 147.

9. For extended discussion, see G. K. Beale, *The Book of Revelation*, New International Greek Testament Commentary (Grand Rapids: Eerdmans, 1999), 153–54.

10. Leon Morris, *The Revelation of St. John,* Tyndale New Testament Commentaries (London: Tyndale, 1969), 22–25; see also Leon Morris, *Apocalyptic* (Grand Rapids: Eerdmans, 1972).

11. See, e.g., the extended discussion in Isbon T. Beckwith, *The Apocalypse of John* (reprint, Grand Rapids: Baker, 1979), 343–93.

12. Extended discussions of these and other introductory matters appear in scholarly commentaries and introductions. See, e.g., Donald Guthrie, *New Testament Introduction*, 4th rev. ed. (Downers Grove, Ill.: InterVarsity, 1990), 929–85.

13. Beckwith, *The Apocalypse of John*, 704–5.

14. Ibid., 705.

15. Suetonius, *Domitian* 12.2.

16. Colin Hemer, *The Letters to the Seven Churches of Asia in Their Local Setting* (Sheffield: JSOT, 1986), 8.

17. C. S. Lewis, *The Lion, the Witch and the Wardrobe* (New York: Macmillan, 1950), 64–65.

18. G. K. Beale, *The Book of Revelation*, New International Greek Testament Commentary (Grand Rapids: Eerdmans, 1999), 298.

19. Much of this interpretation of Daniel 9 I owe to Meredith G. Kline, "The Covenant of the Seventieth Week," in *The Law and the Prophets*, ed. John H. Skilton (Philadelphia: Presbyterian and Reformed, 1974), 452–69.

20. See Beale, *The Book of Revelation*, 635.

21. Beale, *The Book of Revelation*, 718–28.

22. I am indebted to Meredith G. Kline, "The First Resurrection," *Westminster Theological Journal* 37 (1974–75): 366–75, for this line of interpretation.

23. See Beale, *The Book of Revelation*, 1151–53.

Index of Scripture